World of
POLLINATORS
A Guide for Explorers of All Ages

Special Thanks to Our Technical Reviewers:
Brian Cunningham, Wild Birds Unlimited

Robert Frank
BS, Biology & Environmental Science
Environmental Educator
Pennsylvania Watershed and Forest Conservationist

Jennifer L.J. Miller
Commercial Perennial Plant Advisor, Native Plant Specialist

CRE✲TIVE
HOMEOWNER®

Managing Editor: Gretchen Bacon
Editor: Joseph Borden
Designer: Joe Rasemas
Indexer: Jay Kreider
Proofreader: Kurt Heinrich

World of Pollinators
ISBN (softcover): 978-1-58011-596-4
ISBN (hardcover): 978-1-58011-599-5
The Cataloging-in-Publication Data is on file with the Library of Congress.

We are always looking for talented authors. To submit an idea, please send a brief inquiry to acquisitions@foxchapelpublishing.com.

Printed in China

Creative Homeowner®, *www.creativehomeowner.com*, is distributed exclusively in North America by Fox Chapel Publishing Company, Inc., 800-457-9112, 903 Square Street, Mount Joy, PA 17552, and in the United Kingdom by Grantham Book Service, Trent Road, Grantham, Lincolnshire, NG31 7XQ.

World of
POLLINATORS

A Guide for Explorers of All Ages

FOX CHAPEL
PUBLISHING

Introduction

Thread Waist Wasp

Monarch Butterfly

Welcome to the wonderful world of pollinators—a world of buzzing bees, fluttering butterflies, and humming hummingbirds that are not only amazing to watch, but are also extremely important to our survival on Earth.

It's hard to believe, but it's true, the world as we know it would be mostly desert if it weren't for the hard work billions of insects, birds, and small animals do every day on our farms and in our fields, gardens, and forests pollinating the world's greatest resource...plants!

Plants from the largest trees to the tiniest wildflowers provide the world with many important things, including the oxygen we breathe, fruits and vegetables we eat, food for our pets and farm animals, and ingredients for life-saving medicines. Most plants can't survive and produce seeds to grow new plants without pollination, the process in nature that moves very small, powder-sized molecules called pollen from flower blossom to flower blossom.

Although a small number of plants can pollinate on their own with help from the wind, many need the help of insects and animals who transfer pollen as they go from one plant to another. These small insects and animals are called pollinators, the hardest-working creatures in nature.

As the world's human population grows—with more land being used for growing cities, new roads, neighborhoods, parking lots, and factories—less land is available for plants and pollinators. The result is a shrinking population of these important creatures.

Noctuid Moth

Wheel Bug Nymph

Bumblebee

Flower Longhorn Beetle

Tiger Swallowtail

But there's good news! As we learn about the important work pollinators do, people of all ages are planting flowering plants and trees, along with pollinator shelters, to help pollinators survive despite many of the challenges they face today. And no matter where you live, a busy city or out in the country, you can make a difference.

In this book, you'll find a lot of great facts and photos featuring some of the world's most popular and helpful pollinators and the plants they love the most, along with a few simple projects to help feed and protect pollinators.

A simple small patch of wildflowers can attract and feed hundreds of small pollinating insects and animals. The images of pollinators in these pages were all taken within 15 minutes of each other on an early summer day, all visiting a small wildflower garden, some just making a quick stop on their way to a nearby farm or orchard, while some stayed through the season, laying eggs and producing the next generation of pollinators. This little wildflower patch is one very small garden that has become a wonderful food source and shelter for insects and birds, and it will see hundreds of different pollinators visiting throughout the spring, summer, and early fall months.

Whether a small flowerpot on a balcony or small garden in the backyard, pollinators will greatly appreciate your help as they continue their hard work helping to keep our forests, farms, fields, and vegetable gardens healthy and strong year after year.

We thank you for learning about the world of pollinators and doing your part to protect and preserve Earth's most fascinating and important helpers!

Black Swallowtail

Duskywing Skipper

Table of Contents

45

50

14

31

53

56

Table of Contents

60

102

64

97

102

106

137

118

138

All About
Pollen

Close-up of a beautiful purple
tulip bloom full of pollen.

Did You KNOW?

Tulips are considered self-pollinating
plants, meaning they can survive and
make new tulips without their pollen
being transferred to another tulip.

Most people believe that pollen is only yellow in color, but it can be found in many different colors including red, purple, white, and brown. Over thousands of years, flowers have adapted the color of their pollen to attract the insects and animals they need to successfully pollinate every year. For example, insects such as bees can't see red, so many plants produce yellow pollen to attract them. Certain birds and butterflies are attracted to bright red colors, so some plants produce red pollen to attract specific birds and butterflies, which help with their pollination process every year.

Microscopic close-up of a single pollen molecule.

What is pollination?

Pollination is the transfer of pollen—tiny, dust-size particles—either within a flower blossom or between flowers. Pollination is essential for plants to produce seeds. Wind and rain can help move pollen, but birds, bees, butterflies, and other animals and insects play an even more important role. These pollinators visit flowers every day—mostly for sweet nectar—and pick up pollen that they transfer to other flowers without even knowing it!

Pollen is a very fine powder produced by many of the plants around the world, often found in the blossoms of trees and flowers of plants on the ground. Without pollen and the help of animals and insects to move the fine pollen powder from one flower or blossom to another, many of the plants we see every day in our neighborhoods would not be able to reproduce. And without plants, people, our pets, and animals that live in forests and on farms would not have enough food to eat.

DID YOU KNOW?

A single pollen particle is nearly impossible to see without the help of a microscope or powerful magnifying glass. Scientists have learned over the years that each type of plant produces its own unique pollen shape, similar to human fingerprints.

Who invented the microscope?

It's not clear who invented the microscope. Many believe that Hans and Zacharias Janssen, a father-and-son-team of spectacle makers, created the first microscope in 1590. Scientists continued to refine the design over time, using different combinations of lenses and light sources, eventually creating the modern microscopes used today in laboratories around the world.

Most of the pollen that causes allergic reactions comes from trees, grasses, and weeds. These plants make very small, light, and dry pollen grains that travel by the wind. They then can easily find their way into your eyes, nose, and lungs, causing your eyes to itch and nose to run. For some people, spring and early summer are difficult times to breathe easily, as pollen is in the air due to the wind blowing through the forests and flower fields.

Although bees seek out pollen for protein, they also love nectar, which they use as a food source and turn into honey. Bees also use pollen as food for their larvae, which are similar to small grubs at this stage, without legs, wings, or many other features. The pollen is combined with bee saliva to make "bee bread," which is high in the nutrients growing bees need.

Why do bees like pollen?

Bees are hardworking insects and burn up a lot of calories nearly every minute of every day. Pollen is filled with protein, fat, and other nutrients that help bees keep up their energy levels. Bees require both pollen and nectar to survive. Bees also have the amazing ability to turn nectar from flowers into sweet-tasting honey.

An Empress Brilliant Hummingbird sucking sweet nectar from a red flower.

About Flowers

Parts of a Flower

Anther: the part of the stamen that holds the pollen

Stamen: the male part of a flower that produces pollen

Filament: the stalk that holds the anther

Nectar: a naturally occurring sweet liquid found in the glands of many flowers

Close-up of a vibrant tiger lily, a favorite for many hummingbirds and bees.

Photosynthesis

Photosynthesis is the process by which plants use sunlight, water, and carbon dioxide to create energy in the form of sugar, which plants use as food. A byproduct of this process is oxygen, which all animals need to survive. The main function of flower petals is to attract insects for pollination and to protect the reproductive organs located in the center of the flower.

Why are flower petals different for different species?

Petals are essentially modified leaves. Plants have different leaf patterns depending on their strategy for moisture conservation and use of sunlight for photosynthesis.

Petals: the colorful, pretty parts of a flower

Cross-Pollination vs. Self-Pollination

When flowering plants need the assistance of pollinators to transfer the pollen from the stamen to the anther, it is called cross-pollination.

Some flowering plants can self-pollinate, meaning they can use the pollen that they produce without the assistance of bees, butterflies, and bugs. In self-pollinating flowers, the pollen produced by the stamen can fall directly onto the anthers without any help other than a gentle breeze.

True Blue?

Although every color from bright red to black can be found, true-blue flowers are very rare in nature. Some scientists believe a true-blue flower doesn't exist at all due to the lack of blue pigment in the plant world. Often, people mistake shades of purple and violet for blue.

Did You KNOW?

There are over 400,000 flowering plant species across the world, producing a variety of flower types in a range of colors, shades, shapes, and sizes. The shape, size, and color of a flower's petals is the easiest way to identify a flower. The flower's color, shape, and even number of petals are important for pollinators when they decide which flower to visit when looking for nectar or pollen. A flower's petal size and variety depend on the plant's strategy for pollination.

Flower Shapes

Pollinators are attracted to different types of flowers for different reasons, including a flower's color, shape, and the smell of its nectar. Certain insects look for flower blossoms that are easy landing pads, while hummingbirds look for more tube-shaped flowers so they can easily stick their beak and tongue in to suck out the nectar while staying airborne.

1.

2.

3.

4.

5.

6.

7.

1. **Bell shaped.** Bell-shaped flowers, such as the foxglove, have a wide tube and flared petal tips or lobes that vary in length. These are often visited by hummingbirds.

2. **Funnel shaped.** Funnel-shaped flowers have a narrow base and gradually widen in a flared or open shape. One example of these types is the morning glory, a flower visited by bees, small butterflies, and hummingbirds.

3. **Trumpet shaped.** Trumpet-shaped flowers are similar to the end of a trumpet, narrow at the bottom, with the petals opening gently out. Pollinators with long tongues, such as the hummingbird moth, can easily suck out the nectar from these.

4. **Bowl shaped.** Bowl-shaped blooms have a symmetrical, deep-dish shape similar to a cup shape, but deeper. They have straight sides or a slight flare to the tips of the petals. The poppy is one example of this type and is the perfect flower for butterflies and bees.

5. **Saucer shaped.** Saucer-shaped flowers are nearly flat from one side to another, with petal tips that turn slightly upward. Butterflies can easily land on these types of flowers. Great examples of plants with saucer-shaped flowers include geranium, peony, magnolia, and camellia (pictured on the page to the left).

6. **Tubular shaped.** Tubular-shaped flowers have a thin, long tube with straight sides that form their connected petals. They often separate at the mouth of the flower into a flared shape. The lilac is a great example of a tubular flower.

7. **Spherical.** Spherical flowers form an almost-perfect round shape that is made up of one single flower. Globe thistle, peony, and cornflowers are great examples that are must-haves when planting a garden specifically for butterflies.

How Pollen Moves

Cross-Pollination

While there are some plants that can pollinate with help from the wind and rain, many plants need the help of bees and other insects to carry small pollen particles from one plant to another. This is called cross-pollination. If cross-pollination does not happen, a plant will have trouble producing seeds and fruit and eventually will not survive.

Although a bee, for instance, might visit several different types of plants in a day, successful cross-pollination can only happen when a bee transfers pollen from the same type of plant, meaning a bee can't cross-pollinate a rose with a tulip.

Bee

Pollen

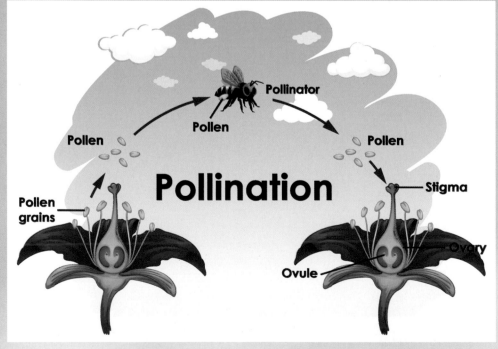

Pollinator

Pollen

Pollen

Pollen

Pollination

Pollen grains

Stigma

Ovary

Ovule

Self-Pollination

Some plants, such as orchids, are self-pollinating and rely on the wind or rain to help transfer pollen within their own blooms. Most self-pollinating plants have tiny flowers that shed pollen directly onto the stigma, sometimes even before the bud opens. Pollinators such as bees, butterflies, and insects will still visit self-pollinating plants for their sweet nectar.

Did You KNOW?

Orchids can be found all around the globe in over 200 countries and on all continents except for Antarctica. There are nearly 25,000 different orchid species around the world.

Close-up of spider orchid flowers.

We Need Plants to Survive!

Plants are the main providers of oxygen on Earth. Without pollinators to help plants cross-pollinate, many plants would not survive, which means our oxygen levels on Earth would not be high enough for people to live. In addition to releasing oxygen, plants also absorb carbon dioxide, which is very important to our survival. Carbon dioxide is a greenhouse gas, and it makes the planet's temperature rise if there's too much of it in the air.

Plants are the main food source for insects, animals, birds, and people. Without plants, many living creatures could not survive. In addition to being a food source, plants and trees provide shelter for thousands of different types of birds, animals, and insects. These critters live in their roots, leaves, stems, and trunks. Researchers have confirmed that a single tree can be the home to over 20,000 different creatures, from tiny, microscopic organisms, butterflies, and moths to large birds and animals.

Without plants, many of the medicines we use today—such as aspirin, which helps with headaches—would not exist. Researchers and scientists continue to work every day in research labs, researching chemicals in plants and how they can help fight sickness and diseases. About 50% of medicines made today use chemicals that come from plants.

How Pollen Moves

Wind

Some crops are not pollinated by insects at all, but instead rely on the wind to help move pollen either inside its own bloom or from one plant to another. A popular vegetable that has this need is sweet corn. Sweet corn pollen is made in the tassels of the corn and needs to be transferred to silks on the ear of the corn for the corn plant to produce edible corn kernels. Farmers plant corn in big fields with many rows alongside each other to help pollen transfer from one plant to another when the wind blows.

A single ear of corn in a cornfield.

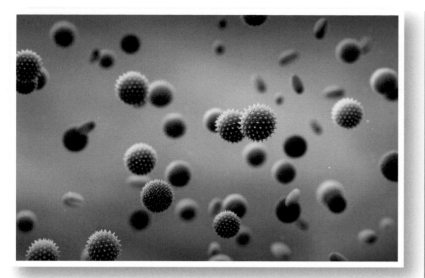

A microscopic view of pollen particles.

Ragweed growing in a field.

How far can pollen travel in the wind?

Grains of pollen can be easily picked up by the wind and carried great distances when conditions are right. Ragweed pollen has been found more than 15,000 feet in the air (nearly three miles or five kilometers) and has been carried as far as 400 miles (640km) from its original place. When the air cools at night and the wind dies, the high-flying pollen drifts back to Earth, landing miles from the plant in which it was produced.

Did You KNOW?

Although there are about 17 types of ragweed in North America, two species are the most abundant. Common ragweed can stand anywhere from a few inches high to 6' (1.8m) tall. Giant ragweed can reach heights of over 18' (5.5m).

A single ragweed plant can produce billions of pollen grains in one season. During the height of the blooming season, vast quantities of pollen are released into the air. You will often notice these grains when they settle on the ground or on the surface of a puddle or pond. If you're walking at this time of year, you might even notice a thin layer of yellow dust on your clothing. The abundance of ragweed during the height of pollination is the reason many people have an allergic reaction to ragweed pollen when it is breathed in on windy days.

By Hand

Hand-pollination is a process developed by people to help plants pollinate when natural pollination can't occur, often when there are not enough pollinators in the area. The most common reasons for a lower number of pollinators are the use of pesticides, which kills insects, and the destruction of pollinators' natural habitats, such as rainforests or flowering meadows. Both of these are usually caused by people, either from cultivating land for farming or development for homes and businesses.

Delicious strawberries grown indoors with the help of hand-pollination.

A small, dry paintbrush is the perfect tool for transferring pollen from one plant to another.

The flower of the zucchini plant in a greenhouse being pollinated manually by the stamens of the male flower.

Why pollinate by hand?

When food growers don't have the help of pollinators in their areas, they can take on the hard task of pollinating by hand or machine. Although hand-pollination can be done with some plants, it is much slower and more difficult than when the task is performed by hardworking bees and insects, who are far better pollinators than people. Hand-pollination is often done with a cotton swab or small brush, but can also be done by removing the petals from a male flower and brushing it against the stigmas of female flowers. With plants that don't need cross-pollination, such as tomatoes, simply shaking the plant can manually pollinate it.

These strawberries are being grown indoors in small bins. These plants were pollinated by hand, without the help of bees or other insects.

By Pollinator

Without pollinators, we would have a very difficult time keeping plants alive. Around the world, more than 300,000 different types of insects such as bees, beetles, wasps, ants, butterflies, and moths play a part in keeping plants alive and producing food that feeds humans and animals alike. There are more than 1,000 different birds and animals, including bats and small mammals, that also help to serve this function.

How many insects are on Earth?

The simple answer is there's no true way to know how many different types of insects live on planet Earth, and it's even more difficult to know how many insects are roaming the planet at any given moment. Some scientists estimate there are about 30 million different types of living insects. New insects continue to be discovered every day in water and on land.

Some scientists believe there are about 10 quintillion (10,000,000,000,000,000,000) individual insects alive at any given moment.

Did You KNOW?

Butterflies come in many shapes and colors. To date, over 17,500 different types of butterflies have been discovered, with around 750 species living in the United States.

Ladybugs

Spider Wasp

Giant Silk Moth

Rufous Hummingbird

A monarch butterfly looks for nectar.

A European hornet feeds on cotoneaster flower nectar.

A honeybee collects pollen from a tree blossom.

Where Pollination Happens
In the Forest

The air around the treetops in the forest during spring is often filled with pollen, creating a hazy appearance.

Most people think pollination only happens with flowers, but did you know trees need pollination, too? Some trees need help from pollinators. Other trees—such as pines, spruce trees, and hemlocks—depend on the wind to help make pollination happen.

Did You KNOW?

Because evergreen trees don't have flowers with nectar and pollen, pine trees don't attract bees, butterflies, and other pollinators; all they need for pollination is wind. The male cones are the ones that produce tiny pollen grains which drift to female cones on other trees.

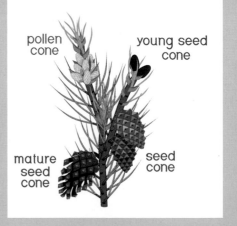

pollen cone

young seed cone

mature seed cone

seed cone

Why do we need trees?

Trees are important to our planet, as they provide oxygen to all living creatures, as well as shelter for insects, birds, and animals. Trees are cut down and used to make many materials, including lumber to build homes and make paper. Over 15 billion trees are cut down annually, with about 5 billion trees being replanted by people each year. It's important that we all continue to recycle to help reduce the number of trees cut down and continue to plant trees and protect our forests.

This small oak tree is only a few inches tall, but the tallest oak trees can reach heights up to 50'–70' (15.3–21.3m) tall.

Did You KNOW?

Researchers believe there are over 73,000 different types of trees around the world. New types of trees are still being discovered. Although hard to count, there are an estimated 3 trillion trees on Earth.

Pollen releasing from a Japanese cedar tree into the air during a windy day.

The world's tallest tree is a 380-foot (115.8m) coast redwood tree named Hyperion. It is located in California's Redwood National Park. Scientists believe the tree is between 600 and 800 years old. In order to protect this tree, people are not allowed to visit it.

Yellow cluster pollen-bearing cones emerge in the spring season on a creeping pine.

Where Pollination Happens
In the City

There are over 50,000 cities on planet Earth, and many continue to grow little by little every year as the world's population grows. More than half the world's population lives in cities, towns, and the built-up areas near them. Although cities are not home to farms, more and more cities are working hard to build flower gardens, plant trees, and build habitats that help pollinators refuel when moving through a heavily populated area.

Create a pollinator pathway!

Adding small flower boxes or hanging planters to your apartment balcony or window ledge will turn a plain space into great resting and refueling stations for bees, butterflies, and hummingbirds.

How do you help pollinators in the city?

Neighborhoods are working together to plant wildflowers along the sidewalks, parking lots, and even on rooftops to help keep our pollinators healthy on their journey to the next destination. City parks, home gardens, planted medians, manicured municipal spaces, rooftop gardens, and even weedy remnants are great pollinator habitats within urban areas.

Even tall buildings can be designed to include room for plants to grow on their window ledges and walls.

Lombard Street in San Francisco is one of the world's most famous streets for its tight, steep turns and beautiful flower gardens.

Lush blooming alyssum growing in a hanging planter on the balcony is the perfect stop for any nearby pollinator.

Even a small patch of what appears to be weeds on a sidewalk will become a place for pollinators to rest and refuel.

Did YOU KNOW?

According to the United Nations, a megacity has a population of 10 million people or more. Currently, there are fewer than 37 megacities in the world, with that number expected to rise to 41 by the year 2030.

Where Pollination Happens
In the Desert

A giant Joshua tree provides a habitat for numerous birds, mammals, insects, and lizards.

A saguaro cactus begins to bloom around the last two weeks of April through the first week in June.

Deserts are very hot and dry places with little rainfall during the year. These areas are so hot that rain often evaporates before it reaches the ground. Hummingbirds, bats, butterflies, bees, and even doves help pollinate plants that live in the desert. Without these helpful animals and insects, many desert plants, like the towering saguaro cactus, cannot produce seeds that are necessary for the cactus to survive. Deserts can also be in the pathway for migrating pollinators (such as the hummingbird) who may not live in the desert, but search for flowering cacti for fresh pollen when traveling through the region.

A bee collects nectar from a cactus.

This purple Santa Rita prickly pear cactus is in full bloom.

Did YOU KNOW?

There are about 2,000 different kinds of cacti around the world. Cacti can take between one and ten years to bloom, but some can take up to 50 years before they start to flower. Some cacti, like most agaves, only bloom once in a lifetime, while others, such as Christmas cacti, bloom every year.

Desert Facts

- A desert receives less than 10 inches (25.4cm) of rain a year.

- Many animals that live in the desert are nocturnal, meaning they only come out at night when it's cooler.

- The Sahara is the largest hot desert on Earth and is located on the continent of Africa. It covers over 3,552,140 square miles (9,200,000 square kilometers).

- Antartica is the largest cold desert on Earth, covering over 5,275,000 square miles (13,662,187 square kilometers).

- Twenty percent of the world's land surface is desert.

This beaver tail cactus with bright pink flowers is a definite stop for any traveling hummingbirds.

Did YOU KNOW?

The Costa's hummingbird has learned to live in the harsh desert environment very well. This hummingbird was named after the French nobleman and naturalist Louis Marie Pantaleon Costa.

A hummingbird flies near blooming saguaro cactus in the Sonoran Desert near Tucson, Arizona.

Where Pollination Happens
On The Farm

All farms require a lot of land and smart farmers who understand what, when, and where to plant. Farmers also understand how important pollination is for their crops and livestock. Without bees and pollination, farms would not be able to grow many of the crops important to keep the world's population healthy and strong.

Most farms fall into one of three different types: arable, pastoral, or mixed.

Arable farms produce food crops, everything from carrots and lettuce to corn and wheat. Depending on the location and climate, some arable farms work all year long while others are busiest during the warmer months only.

Pastoral farms are designed to raise livestock such as cows, sheep, and goats. Raising animals is a job that runs 24 hours a day and 365 days a year.

Mixed farms do both, growing vegetables and raising livestock.

Did You KNOW ?

Pollinators are responsible for at least 1 of every 3 bites of food we eat every single day.

Cows and livestock eat feed that doesn't grow unless pollination occurs.

Did You KNOW ?

An average adult cow will consume about 2 percent of its body weight or 24 pounds (10.9kg) of grasses and grains every day.

Corn

Cucumber

Green Beans

Alfalfa

Cucumbers and zucchini need the help of pollinators to grow.

Many of our favorite vegetables and fruits, from watermelon to cucumbers, require the help of pollinators. Some vegetables, such as green peppers, green beans, and lima beans, and crops, such as wheat and rice, self-pollinate. Pollination still occurs but insects are not needed. There are also many vegetable plants that require cross-pollination.

Corn is a vegetable that requires cross-pollination by wind-blown pollen from the flowers or tassels at the top of the plant to the flowers or silks about midway up the stalks. Each kernel develops from an individually pollinated silk. Corn is planted in side-by-side rows to help pollination when the wind blows. A single row of corn will have less chance of successful pollination.

Cucumbers are highly dependent on bees and insects to help with pollination. Millions of cucumbers are produced every year with smaller varieties made into pickles. An average cucumber plant can be expected to produce at least 10 large cucumbers in a season while the smaller types used for pickles can produce over 50 small cucumbers per plant. Farmers who specialize in vegetables such as cucumbers often keep beehives near their fields.

Green beans, like green peppers and lima beans, are self-pollinating, meaning that pollen from the same plant can be received by that plant and used to grow.

Alfalfa is an important food for dairy cattle that helps them produce the great-tasting milk we use in everything from ice cream to our morning cereal. Alfalfa needs the assistance of bees in order to grow year after year.

Eating Roots!

When you eat certain vegetables like carrots, beets, and potatoes, you're actually eating the root of the plant. These types of vegetables are called root vegetables and do not need the help of pollinators to produce the part we eat, which is underground. But don't think root vegetables don't need pollination to survive. The plant part of a root vegetable that grows above ground will produce flowers and needs help from pollinators to produce seeds for the next generation of carrots, turnips, sweet potatoes, etc.

Did **You** KNOW **?**

Leafy greens such as lettuce and spinach, as well as crops like broccoli and cauliflower, do not need pollination to occur to produce the part we eat. However, they do need pollination for the plants to produce seeds.

Carrots are a favorite for small pollinators. Carrot tops, when fully grown, will produce tiny white flowers that are full of nectar and easy for small bees, ladybugs, and other insects to reach. When in full bloom, a carrot patch will be a buzz of pollinator activity.

When in bloom, celery tops are another plant full of nectar and are highly attractive to bees.

Grow your own tomatoes!

Tomato plants are a great addition to a small pollinator garden, either in the backyard or on the balcony. Their tiny yellow flowers are a great source of nectar and pollen for bees and butterflies. Tomatoes are also easy to grow if you have plenty of sun. Be sure to read your seed packet or instructions if you buy small starter plants. Some tomato plants are more like a vine and will need stakes to climb up, while others have short, stocky plants.

Tomato plants are considered self-pollinating, containing both the stamen and stigma in the same flower. Although wind can help a tomato plant self-pollinate, bees such as the carpenter bee and bumblebee can greatly help the pollination process when they grab the center of the flower and shake lots of pollen loose.

Tomatoes are the main ingredient in many of our favorite foods, from the sauce used in spaghetti or pizza to many types of chili and soups. Tomatoes are also the main ingredient of ketchup, which can be found in many homes and restaurants around the world. Heinz®, a big ketchup manufacturer, uses 2 million tons of tomatoes every year.

There are more than 10,000 different types of tomatoes. They come in many different colors including red, orange, pink, and purple.

Beefsteak tomatoes are some of the largest cultivated tomatoes.

Did You KNOW?

A giant pumpkin can grow 100 times faster than typical pumpkins. In just a single day, they can gain an average of 20–40lb (9.1–18.1kg).

Where Pollination Happens
In the Orchard

An orchard is a type of farm where fruits and nuts are grown on trees and shrubs. Examples of orchard fruits are apples, pears, oranges, bananas, and cherries. Examples of orchard nuts are pecans, walnuts, and almonds.

No Bees, No Apples

Without bees, most apple trees would not produce any apples at all. The pollen from a tree's flowers will not pollinate other flowers on the same tree. Trees need bees to help carry pollen from another tree to produce their fruit.

Orchard growers are always watching the number of bees and other pollinators working in their orchards. They will go to great lengths to keep their bees safe and happy and will also work with professional bee handlers to bring in extra bees during the early parts of the year when pollination is very important to producing high-quality fruit later in the summer and early fall months.

Did You KNOW ?

Grapevines can self-pollinate and don't need the help of pollinators to produce grapes. But most grape vineyards are surrounded by cover crops, many of which require the help of pollinators to grow. Cover crops such as mustard plants and grain plants (like barley) are planted to help keep soil from washing away when it rains, and they help keep the soil full of nutrients.

How many orchards are there in the world?

There are an estimated 2.2 million fruit tree orchards in the world, with a collective 37 billion fruit trees.

How much pollen do bees spread?

A single colony of bees can successfully pollinate 1–2 acres of land filled with fruit trees and vegetable plants.

A group of worker bees working hard to collect pollen and nectar from pear blossoms.

Bats are wild about bananas!

Bats are very important to the pollination process for wild bananas, which are not the same as bananas you see at your local grocery store. Wild bananas are typically smaller and have larger seeds but can be eaten. Bats and birds help pollinate wild bananas when gathering nectar from the banana blossom and carrying and dropping seeds when they leave the banana plant.

Did You KNOW ?

The wooden box made to house a colony of bees is called an apiary. Honeybees work in the field, bring back pollen to the apiary, and turn it into honey. A bee yard is the place where all the apiaries (which are full of bees) and bee-keeping equipment are kept. These are located near the orchard fields. The average size of a beehive can range from 20,000–60,000 bees.

A row of man-made beehives placed near an orchard.

Our Favorite Foods—Courtesy of
Pollinators

If you imagined a world without bees and other hardworking pollinators, it would be a very different place! Far fewer farms, vegetable gardens, and orchards growing the many wonderful fruits and vegetables we eat every day would not exist. Here are some of our favorite foods that are not possible without help from bees and other pollinator insects.

Sweet Potato Fries

Blueberries

Strawberries

Jack-O'-Lanterns

French Fries

Peaches

Mustard

Cherries

Cauliflower

Carrots

Cranberries

Onions

Radishes

Apples

Pickles

Cantaloupe

Cole Slaw

Raspberries

Watermelon

Wildflowers

Wildflowers are, as the names implies, flowers that grow in the wild, not planted by people. Scientists can tell from fossil records that wildflowers have been on Earth for millions of years. It wasn't until around 300 B.C. that the first recordkeeping of flowers was started by Greek botanist Theophrastus. From what research can tell, this was the first time flowers were studied and named, and he named more than 500 plants. Thanks to work begun by Theophrastus, Romans began to experiment with different types of plants around 23 B.C. and started to understand the benefits and healing power of flowers.

What's the difference between native plants and invasive plants?

Native plants grow naturally in an area for thousands of years and have developed special characteristics that help them not only survive the climate and terrain, but also help the pollinators in that area.

This invasive ivy has taken over the forest, covering all the trees and ground, making it difficult for insects and pollinators to survive.

Invasive plants are often plants brought in from another part of the country or from a different country that are nice to look at but can outcompete the good plants that pollinators need in that area to survive.

Today, many gardening stores and gardening clubs in your community will help when selecting plants so you know which are natives and which plants will be harmful to other plants or not helpful in attracting and keeping pollinators healthy and productive.

Perennial plants regrow every spring, while annual plants live for only one growing season, then die off. Perennials generally have a shorter blooming period compared to annuals, so it's common for gardeners to use a combination of both plants.

Wild orchid near an ancient Inca trail in Cuzco in southern Peru.

On a single day in summer, one acre of wildflower meadow can contain 3 million flowers and produce 2.2lb (1 kg) of nectar sugar for pollinators.

Did YOU KNOW?

There are an estimated 400,000 different types of flowering plants around the world, and millions in total when you count the many variations by color and size. Flowering plants are found on every continent on the planet, including Antarctica, where you will find tiny yellow flowers on the Antarctic pearlwort, commonly found in rocky areas in the coastal regions of the continent. As there are no bees in Antarctica, the pearlwort can self-pollinate with help from the wind.

The Black-Eyed Susan

The black-eyed Susan is one of the most popular wildflower plants in North America. It is easy to grow and is an excellent addition to any flower garden. It's guaranteed to attract butterflies, bees, and many other pollinating insects.

One Tough Flower

Black-eyed Susans are a hardy flower. In the wild, they are often one of the first flowering plants to grow back in an area damaged by fire or natural disasters.

A metallic green sweat bee on a black-eyed Susan.

A red admiral butterfly getting nectar from a patch of black-eyed Susan flowers.

Did YOU KNOW ?

There are over 40 different types of black-eyed Susans, and they can be found in many shades of yellow, orange, orange-red, and shades of gold. They can reach heights between 3'–6' (91.4–182.9cm) feet tall. They produce beautiful, nectar-filled blooms from June to October.

A pink-edged sulphur butterfly gathering nectar from a black-eyed Susan flower in a wildflower meadow.

A crimson black-eyed Susan in Munich, Germany.

The Sunflower

The sunflower is a grand flower that can be found in over 80 countries and is a favorite of pollinators seeking its rich nectar. Sunflowers often tower high above neighboring plants and are most famous for their ability to track the sun, facing east as the sun rises and following the sun as the Earth moves during the day.

Native to the Americas, sunflowers have been used for medicines, dyes, and oils for hundreds of years. These towering flowers were introduced to Europe by Spanish explorers in the 1500s, who discovered them when visiting what is now the Americas.

Did You KNOW?

Although the sunflower blossom appears to be one giant flower, it's actually made up of tiny flowers called florets. Some sunflowers have nearly 2,000 florets!

How do sunflowers pollinate?

Sunflowers can self-pollinate but are more likely to cross-pollinate with the help of bees. Sunflower pollen is very thick and heavy and is picked up by pollinators and transferred from one plant to another.

Sunflowers in Space

In 2012, US astronaut Don Petit transported sunflower seeds to the International Space Station as part of a plant-growing experiment in space!

That's really tall!

The tallest sunflower measures 30' (9.1m) and was grown by Hans-Peter Schiffer in Karst, Nordrhein Westfalen, Germany.

Bees

Buttercup

Possible colors: red, pink, and yellow
Size: 12"–36" (30.5–91.4cm) tall

Crocus

Possible colors: purple, yellow, lavender, cream, and white **Size:** 4"–5" (10.2–12.7cm) tall

Did You KNOW ?

Bees are attracted to thousands of colorful plants in every shape and size. They are most attracted to plants that are purple, violet, and yellow, but they don't like dark colors (including red, which appears black to them). If you want to attract honeybees and bumblebees, stick with lighter colors in your garden. They also like flowers they can fly in and out of easily.

Clover

Possible colors: white, pink, red, or yellow **Size:** 4"–6" (10.2–15.2cm) tall

Dahlia

Possible colors: creamy white to the palest pink, sunny yellow to regal purple, crimson red to (almost) black, and everything in between **Size:** 15"–72" (38.1–182.9cm) tall

Foxglove

Possible colors: pink, cream, rose, purple, white, and primrose **Size:** can reach up to 5' (152.4cm) tall

Geranium

Possible colors: red, white, pink, violet, lilac, apricot, orange, and yellow **Size:** 4"–48" (10.2–121.9cm) tall

Do bees fly in the rain?

Honeybees can fly in a light rain, but they prefer not to. They usually stay inside the hive until the rain passes and it clears up. Bees are also very solar-oriented beings and use the sun for navigation.

A bumblebee collecting nectar in the rain.

Grape Hyacinth

Possible colors: lilacs, pink, white, cobalt blue, cream, apricot **Size:** 8"–10" (20.3–25.4cm) tall

Marigold

Possible colors: orange, golden yellow, and white **Size:** 6"–36" (15.2–91.4cm) tall

Poppy

Possible colors: translucent white through ivory, yellow, gold, orange, and red, shades of blue and purple **Size:** 24"–36" (61–91.4cm) tall

Rhododendron

Possible colors: white, red, pink, yellow, almost blue, purple, magenta, orange, and shades and mixtures of most of these colors **Size:** 3'–8' (91.4–243.8cm) tall

Sunflower

Zinnia

Possible colors: cream to gold, yellow, orange, red, mahogany, and chocolate brown **Size:** can reach up to 16' (4.9m) tall

Possible colors: pink, red, purple, orange, yellow, lavender, white, and green **Size:** 12"–48" (30.5–121.9cm) tall

12 Flowers That Attract
Butterflies

Zinnia

Possible colors: pink, red, purple, orange, yellow, lavender, white, and even green. **Size:** 12"–48" (30.5–121.9cm) tall

Purple Coneflower

Color: purple **Size:** 24"–48" (61–121.9cm) tall

Scabiosa

Possible colors: red, purple, lavender, pink, blue, and white **Size:** 12"–18" (30.5–45.7cm) tall

Phlox

Possible colors: range from white and soft pastels to brilliant shades of yellow, red, orange, and gold **Size:** 24"–48" (61–121.9cm) tall

Yarrow

Possible colors: pink, rose, red, lavender, purple, orange, and white **Size:** 24"–36" (61–91.4cm) tall

Stonecrop

Possible colors: range of oranges, reds, greens, blues, and purples **Size:** 16"–18" (40.6–45.7cm) tall

Aster
Possible colors: white, purple, blue, or pink **Size:** 1'–6' (30.5–182.9cm) tall

Cosmos

Possible colors: pink, orange, red, yellow, white, and maroon **Size:** can reach 6' (182.9cm) tall

Bee balm

Goldenrod

Possible colors: red or purple **Size:** 24"–48" (61–121.9cm) tall

Possible colors: yellow or gold **Size:** 2'–6' (61–182.9cm) tall

Did You KNOW?

Butterflies are looking for good landing pads! They are more likely to spend time on flowers that have flat tops, so they can easily perch on them while they feed. These flowers provide a safe place where butterflies can land, rest, and bask in the sun, too.

Liatris

Marigold

Possible colors: orange, golden yellow, and white **Size:** 6"–36" (15.2–91.4cm) tall

Possible colors: usually purple, though there are also some with pink or white flowers **Size:** 1'–5' (30.5–152.4cm) tall

Flowers That Attract
Hummingbirds

Hummingbirds are constantly seeking not only nectar-producing flowers but also flowers that allow for easy hovering while they eat. The flowers pictured are just some of hummingbirds' favorites.

Petunia

Possible colors: many colors; most popular are pink, purple, white, red, yellow, or mixed **Size:** 6"–18" (15.2–45.7cm) tall

Cardinal Flower

Color: brilliant red **Size:** 36"–48" (91.4–121.9cm) tall

How do hummingbirds eat?

Hummingbirds insert their long beaks into flower blossoms and use their forked or grooved tongues to bring the nectar back to their beak and throat. They move their tongue in and out of their slender beak about 13 times per second!

Hummingbird Mint

Possible colors: orange, pink, and red
Size: up to 36" (91.4cm) tall

Honeysuckle

Possible colors: bright pinks, oranges, yellows, or whites
Size: vines can reach up to 30' (9.1m) long

Columbine

Possible colors: purple, red, yellow, pink, and blue

Size: 12"–36" (30.5–91.4cm) tall

Indian Pink

Color: brilliant red **Size:** 12"–18" (30.5–45.7cm) tall

Lupine

Possible colors: usually blue, but can also be white, yellow, or with some species, even red

Size: 12"–36" (30.5–91.4cm) tall

Zinnia

Possible colors: pink, red, purple, orange, yellow, lavender, white, and even green

Size: 12"–48" (30.5–121.9cm) tall

Do hummingbirds have a favorite color?

Although hummingbirds are attracted to many bright colors, red is the clear favorite. Duller colors like violets do not attract them as much.

Making a
Pollination Station

You don't need a backyard or need to live in the country to attract and help pollinators. Even in the busiest of cities, you can provide wonderful flower stations in a simple 10" (25.4cm) pot. Your flowers can be a wonderful rest station for a passing butterfly, bee, insect, or hummingbird on its way to a nearby farm where it will do important work helping our farms and orchards.

Preparation before you begin: Decide which pollinators—bees, butterflies, or hummingbirds—you want to attract. This choice determines which types of plants you want to grow. Remember to think about which colors and flower types will attract the type of pollinators you chose. Hummingbirds love long, tubular, bright flowers, while butterflies need blossoms that are more open and easy to land on. Although flowers in bloom can be bought at your local stores in the spring, options are often limited and not always a good match for pollinators. Starting from seed is easy and will provide hundreds of flowering options and a wonderful way to learn about plants.

You will need:

- Terra cotta pot at least 10" (25.4cm) across the top and at least 8" (20.3cm) deep with drainage holes in the bottom (Plastic pots will work if terra cotta is not available)
- Saucer for under your pot to avoid water damage to surface underneath
- Small bag of potting soil (a 20lb. [9.1kg] bag will fill four to six 10" [25.4cm] pots)
- A few small stones
- Craft stick
- Seeds of your choice
- Piece of blank white paper

Step 1. Place several small stones in the bottom to help water drain.

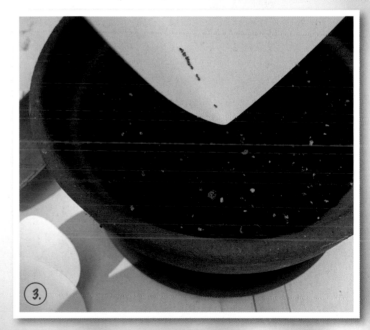

Step 2. Use a small shovel or your hands to fill your pot with potting soil, leaving about 1" (3.8cm) from the top open.

Step 3. Scatter your seeds on the top, following the directions on the packet of seeds you chose. If your seeds are very tiny, fold a piece of white paper and gently drop the seeds around the top surface by tapping the paper to help the seeds move down the fold and fall into the soil.

4.

5.

Step 5. Add a little water, just enough for the surface to get wet. How often you need to water your flowerpot will depend on the dryness of the surface. In order for your seeds to grow, avoid the soil drying out. Check the surface of the soil every 3 to 4 days. You will see little sprouts emerging with the first week or two. Times will vary depending on the type of flower you've planted.

Step 4. Using your hands, gently scatter a layer of topsoil over the seeds. Your seed packet instructions will tell you how much soil to place on top of the seeds. Most flowers require ¼" (6.4mm) to ½" (1.3cm).

6.

7.

Step 6. Using a craft stick, write down the name of the seeds you've planted and place it in the pot near the edge. Marking each pot just after planting the seeds will help keep your pollination stations organized, especially if you decide to plant multiple stations.

Step 7. Place your pot in an outdoor setting that gives the proper amount of sun per the instructions on your seed packet.

A western swallowtail in a pot of native zinnias.

Even a single small zinnia flower can be a welcome sight to a passing butterfly or bee.

A collection of flowers such as this can be a huge help to pollinators.

All About
Bees and Wasps

Wings

Compound eye

Thorax

Antenna

Abdomen

Head

Legs

bumblebee   wasp

There are an estimated 20,000 species of bees, classified into nine distinct families, which can be divided into three broad groups according to the average length of the bee's tongue, or what is called a proboscis. The long-tongued bees sip nectar from deep within the floral chambers, while the shorter-tongued bees tend to more closely resemble their carnivorous wasp ancestors.

How can you tell a bee from a wasp?

Bees are rounder with fuller bodies, thicker legs, and fuzzy hairs. These hairs help them collect pollen and carry it back to the hive. Wasps are slimmer, have narrow waists, and have thin legs. Their bodies are smooth and shiny without hairs on them.

Bees also lose their stinger when they sting, which causes them to die. A wasp can sting multiple times. Another key difference is wasps and bees live in different-sized colonies. Honeybee colonies can have populations over 75,000, while wasps' colonies tend to have fewer than 10,000.

Did You KNOW ?

Most wasps will hibernate during the winter season and build a new nest the following autumn. Honeybees do not hibernate, as they live on food reserves and heat accumulated by thousands of workers.

ANATOMY OF A BEE

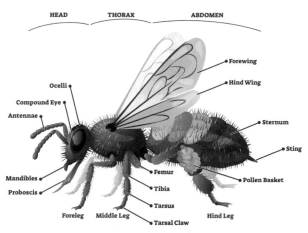

HEAD   THORAX   ABDOMEN

Ocelli
Compound Eye
Antennae
Mandibles
Proboscis
Foreleg   Middle Leg
Femur
Tibia
Tarsus
Tarsal Claw
Hind Leg
Forewing
Hind Wing
Sternum
Sting
Pollen Basket

Can you outrun a bee?

A bee can reach speeds between 12 and 15 mph (19.3 and 24.1 kph). So, if you're in good shape, it's possible to outrun a bee, as long as you keep running!

Do bees want to sting you?

Bees do not want to sting you and only sting as a form of defense. This is especially true for very calm bees like honeybees. But they are very passionate about protecting their family. They will give everything they have to ward off an attacker.

Although it's natural to be nervous when a bee lands you, don't swat them away, as this will make them angry and more likely to sting you. Don't panic, as it's probably just trying to smell you and it'll move on soon. If it doesn't fly away, blow gently on it to encourage it to leave.

Where do bees live?

Believe it or not, most bees, wasps, and hornets actually nest underground. If you've seen wasp activity around your house but can't find the nest, then these pests might be nesting underground.

Some bee-like hornets produce a paper-like material to build nests that they hang from trees or under areas of a house roof or barn, which helps protect them from the weather.

Honeybees can thrive in natural or domesticated environments, though they prefer to live in gardens, woodlands, orchards, meadows, and other areas where flowering plants are abundant. Within their natural habitat, honeybees build nests inside tree cavities and under edges of objects to hide themselves from predators.

Wasps

Cicada killers. Despite their large size and bright yellow stripes, cicada killers are harmless to humans. They're considered gentle giants of the wasp world, and unlike Asian giant hornets, female cicada killers avoid people and rarely deploy their stingers. Adults will feed on flower nectar, sap from trees, and other large plants in their habitat.

Hornets. Hornets are a type of wasp and are not always easy to identify. They're bigger than their wasp cousins and are more commonly found in Asia, but they do exist in other parts of the world including North American, Europe, and Africa. Not all hornets are known to be good pollinators, except for the bald-faced hornet, who visits flowers for their sweet nectar during the hot summer months.

Mud daubers. As their name suggests, mud daubers build their nests out of mud, usually in shady areas under a porch, wood pile, or machinery. A mud dauber's favorite food is flower nectar and spiders.

Paper wasps. Paper wasps get their name from the paper-like material with which they make their nests. Paper wasps are sometimes called umbrella wasps, after the shape of their distinctive nests.

Yellow jackets. Yellow jackets love sugar and will quickly find an open can of soda or sweet-smelling perfume. Although yellow jackets will also visit nectar-filled flowers, they are carnivorous and eat small insects.

Bees

Bumblebees. Bumblebees are very peaceful and not aggressive, even when compared to the pleasant nature of honeybees. Most bumblebees live in underground hives in holes made by larger animals.

Carpenter bees. Most bees live together in groups called hives. However, carpenter bees are considered solitary bees because they don't work or live in colonies. Both male and female carpenter bees hibernate alone, most often in previously built brood tunnels where they have stored a small amount of pollen to withstand the colder temperatures.

European dark bee. The European dark bee is a larger honeybee. Like many bees, its population is shrinking. The European dark bee is mostly found in the UK and is well suited for cooler, rainy climates.

Leafcutter bees. Leafcutter bees get their nickname from what they do: cut leaves. They use these cuttings to build chambers for their eggs. They will pollinate most flowering garden vegetables and flowers including alfalfa, carrots, blueberries, cranberries, legumes, melons, onions, and peas. They are such good pollinators that they are often used by farmers for commercial pollination.

Mason bees. Mason bees are some of the first bees to emerge in the spring and are excellent pollinators. They can tolerate colder temperatures as low as 55 degrees Fahrenheit (12.8°C). For much of North America, this means that mason bees will be active beginning in late February to early April.

Mining bee. Mining bees are common and often found nesting in lawns. They are masters at excavating holes in the ground for their nests. They are often mistaken for bumblebees, and like bumblebees, they are not aggressive and typically do not sting. They are very important to flower pollination, especially in the Midwest region of the United States.

Amazing Honeybees

Did You KNOW?

Honeybees are very social insects and live in huge groups called colonies. A single colony will have one queen bee, hundreds of drone bees, and between 20,000 and 60,000 female worker bees.

The queen is the largest bee in the honeybee hive. She can lay up to 2,000 eggs per day, which is around twice her body weight.

Hardworking Bees!

Worker bees work nearly 24 hours a day foraging for food, storing honey, and building combs.

Did **You** **KNOW**?

There are over 20,000 different types of bees found throughout the world, including many different types of honeybees.

The Honeybee

Honeybees are incredibly important pollinators for flowering plants and fruit and vegetable plants. Nearly one-third of the fruits and vegetables we consume is the direct result of honeybee pollination.

Parts of the Honeybee

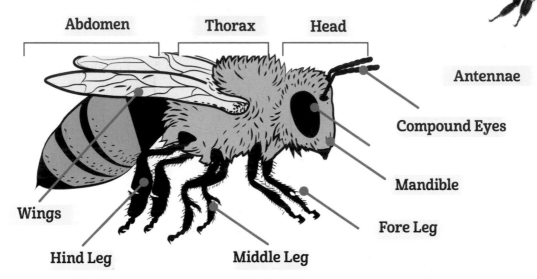

Abdomen

Thorax

Head

Antennae

Compound Eyes

Mandible

Fore Leg

Wings

Hind Leg

Middle Leg

Did You KNOW?

Honeybees have been discovered in fossils in Europe dating back 35 million years ago. Scientists believe they first originated in eastern Africa. After thousands of years, they are now found throughout the world.

How much honey do bees make?

Honeybees have a short life span because they are always working and rarely sleep. Most live between 4–6 weeks. However, the queen bee can live up to two years.

An average worker bee produces ½ of a teaspoon of honey in their lifetime, which is about 6 to 8 weeks. To make one pound of honey, over 500 worker bees must visit over 2 million flowers to gather enough nectar! A honeybee can pollinate between 50 to 100 plants before returning to the hive.

Where does honey get its flavor?

The flavor, smell, and appearance of honey are determined by the kinds of flowers visited by the bees that create it.

How fast can honeybees fly?

Honeybees can fly at an average speed of 15 mph (24.1kph). Their speed can be 20 mph (32.2kph) if they're not carrying a full load of pollen back to the hive. They can flap their wings over 200 times per second.

Bees are heavy lifters!

A single bee can bring back a pollen load that weighs about 35 percent of its body weight. Honeybees carry pollen on their hind legs on areas commonly called the "pollen basket." When you see a honey bee with pollen on its rear legs in flight, you know it's heading back to the hive.

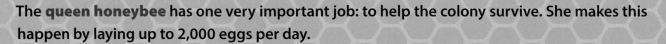

What jobs do honeybees have?

The members of the hive are divided into three types:

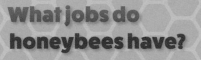

Queen · Worker · Drone

The **queen honeybee** has one very important job: to help the colony survive. She makes this happen by laying up to 2,000 eggs per day.

At least 95% of the hive consists of **worker bees**. In a hive with 60,000 bees, this means 57,000 of them will be worker bees. Worker bees do all the heavy lifting. Some of their duties include taking care of and feeding the young, collecting nectar or processing it as it comes into the hive, feeding the queen, or making honey.

Worker bees are all female. Unlike the queen bee, they can't lay fertilized eggs.

Besides the workers and the queen, a few hundred **drones** are usually part of a colony. A drone is a male honeybee. Unlike the female worker bee, drones do not have stingers. They gather neither nectar nor pollen and are unable to feed without assistance from worker bees. A drone's only role is to mate with an unfertilized queen. Drones are haploid (having only one set of chromosomes), growing from unfertilized eggs by arrhenotoky (a process of reproduction that usually does not involve fusion with another haploid).

How many bees?

The exact number of bees in a colony is hard to determine because it depends on various factors, the most important of which are seasonal variations.

How do bees communicate?

A foraging bee that has just discovered a great source of nectar needs to be able to tell the other workers where to find it. She does it by dancing!

If the flowers are within 30 yards (27.4m), the bee will do a "round dance." The bee flies around in a circle and when she's made a complete circuit, she reverses direction and flies around again. She continues to reverse direction after each circuit. The other bees also pick up the scent of the flowers from the dancing bee, so they know the scent of the flower they need to look for. The "waggle dance" is done when the new nectar hot spot is more than 30 yards (27.4m) away.

Honeybee Dance Movements

Round Dance

Waggle Dance

Why do bees build hexagons?

Over time, the honeybee has learned that a hexagon shape eliminates wasted space and maximizes space for living and storage. A beehive needs to have space for more than 50,000 bees, honey production, and pollen storage in addition to a place to raise young bees.

The Bumblebee

Bumblebees are important pollinators and can be found almost anywhere. You might think of bumblebees as sporting black and yellow stripes, but they can also be orange with white stripes. So, if you're ever trying to find one, look for those colors and a fuzzy body.

Did YOU KNOW?

The world's largest bumblebee lives in South America. This species is called *Bombus dahlbomii*. They are so big and furry that they are often called "flying mice."

A Big Appetite

Bumblebees have such fast metabolisms that they are always about 40 minutes away from starving, even when they're full! That's why they must eat so frequently.

Where do bumblebees live?

Most bumblebees nest in hives in underground holes made by larger animals, while some nest aboveground in abandoned bird nests or cavities such as hollow logs and spaces beneath rocks.

Do bumblebees sting?

Only female bumblebees have stingers. Plus, these bees are not aggressive. Unless you threaten a bee or its nest, it is unlikely it will sting you.

A male red mason bee.

Cool Bees

Bumblebees cool down their nests by flapping their wings. They can flap their wings up to 200 times per second. This technique, called fanning, can greatly cool the heat inside their nests.

What flowers do bumblebees like?

Bumblebees are picky about the flowers they will select for nectar collection. They are most attracted to flowers that are blue or violet and will often overlook flowers of other colors in favor of these.

Did You KNOW ?

Bumblebees have five eyes. The three smaller eyes are located on top of their heads, while the other two are up front. They can see UV light, but they can't see the color red!

The Mason Bee

An adult mason bee.

Mason bees are excellent pollinators, possibly one of the best. They are not known as very graceful flyers and will land on a flower, bumping back and forth into the petals, spreading pollen everywhere. The pollen sticks all over the bee's body, making it more likely to be spread to other nearby flowers. They are more successful at pollenating than most other bees.

Did You KNOW?

Mason bees are fast-moving and efficient pollinators; 250 blue orchard bees (a type of mason bee) can pollinate one acre of apples as effectively as 40,000 honeybees. They also like maple trees. A single mason bee will visit between 1,600 to 2,400 blossoms daily and pollinate over 90% of them.

Where do mason bees live?

Mason bees use holes in dead wood left by beetles and other insects. They'll also use a bee box you can put up in the yard or garden.

What do mason bees look like?

Mason bees commonly have metallic green or blue bodies with sparse hairy patches. Adult mason bees are about ½" (1.2 cm) long with large wings and six hairy, black legs. Mason bees are often confused with houseflies, as they look like a blue housefly. To determine if you've got a fly or bee in your house, simply listen. Houseflies make a humming sound, while mason bees make a buzzing sound.

Why are they called mason bees?

Mason bees get their name from their ability to use masonry type materials such as mud to construct their nests.

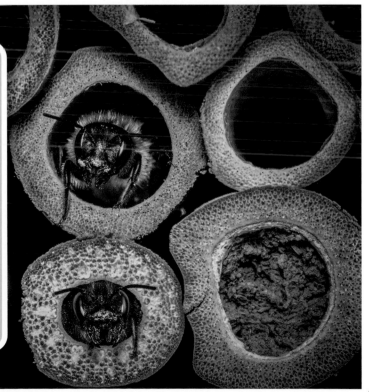

Did YOU KNOW ?

Mason bees are very gentle, solitary pollinators and native to most parts of North America. Between their gentle nature and great ability to pollinate, they make perfect garden guests for people with fruit trees, flowers, and vegetable gardens. To attract mason bees and keep them happy, they need access to a nest, flowers for food, and a mud source.

Building a
Soup Can Bee House

Bee houses are very helpful and will increase pollinators in your garden or next to your pollinator stations. There are several types of bees, including mason bees and leafcutter bees, that look for small, hollow holes in wood, hollow stems, or small holes in manmade structures where they lay their eggs. Making a soup can bee house is an easy and fun project, but most importantly, a great way to help protect and grow your bee pollinator population. Prepare for the spring season by making several bee houses over the winter months. Your bee houses should be put outside in very early spring.

You will need:

- Soup cans
- A nail
- Black coated wire
- Spray paint (tan, grey, or green)
- Small metal rod or extra heavy wire
- Bamboo (about 12' [365.7cm] of bamboo for each 6" (15.2cm), large-size soup can). Bamboo inside the opening should be between ¹⁄₁₆" and ³⁄₈" (1.6 and 9.5mm).
- Hammer
- Hacksaw (or saw with thin, small-toothed blade)

Step 2. With your extra-heavy wire or thin metal rod, push out the center of the bamboo pieces.

Step 1. Cut 24 pieces of different diameter bamboo to the length of the can's inside.

Step 3. Prepare the cans for painting. Take off any labels. Thoroughly wash and dry the inside and outside.

Step 4. Place cans on a piece of paper with the open end down. Apply a coat of paint evenly on all sides. Use an earth tone color that best matches your outdoor environment (such as tan, green, or grey), as this will help your bee house blend in. Avoid bright colors such as red.

(5.)

Step 5. After the paint has dried, use a nail to punch a few very small holes in the can's bottom. These will help keep the inside of the can dry.

(6.)

Step 6. With the can on its side, start placing pieces of bamboo into the can until it's full.

Step 7. Place your bee house at least 4'–6' (1.2–1.8m) off the ground and facing the sun. Attach your bee house to a post, building, or isolated tree. Mount the nest boxes firmly so they do not move or shake in the wind, as movement may disturb developing larvae. Be sure that there are flowering plants nearby that bloom in early spring and throughout the summer. ➡

A bee house attached to a fence post.

Mason bees working hard building nests in tubes.

Make a
Pollinator Water Station

Many people recognize the importance of providing food and shelter for bees, birds, and other pollinators. But pollinators, like all of us, need water to survive and thrive! You can help pollinators by building a simple watering station in your backyard or garden.

You will need:

- A shallow clay saucer
- Small stones and pebbles
- Water

Step 1. Place several small rocks into the saucer. Arrange them so there is a bit of space between each.

Step 2. Loosely fill the remaining spaces with very small pebbles. The rocks and pebbles allow bees to perch and have safe footing from which to drink.

Step 3. Fill the saucer with water.

Step 4. Place the station at ground level near plants that attract pollinators.

Make a
Bug Hotel

Although bees and bugs are very capable of finding their homes in nature, as they have done for millions of years, bug houses have become more important to help pollinators find a place near their food source. As more land is being developed, bugs and bees are challenged more every year to find a home close to pollinating plants during the spring and summer months.

Giving your pollinators an easy-to-find home within feet of your flowering plants and vegetables is a great way keep pollinators nearby, making life a little easier for our tiny pollinating bugs and bees.

There are many designs for bug houses. No design is better than the other, but to attract a lot of different types of pollinating bees and beetles, a bug house should include a range of natural materials and have different compartments for different types and sizes of insects. This four-compartment bug hotel is made of all-natural materials, requires only a few tools, and can be easily placed against a shed wall, a pole, or a table near your garden.

You will need:

- Two 6" x 6' x 1" (15.2 x 182.9 x 2.5cm) white pine boards, untreated
- 20' (6.1m) of bamboo
- 12" x 6" (30.5 x 15.2cm) log
- A collection of tree bark, pinecones, and small twigs
- 12" (30.5cm) piece of dried log; oak, ash, and beech are good choices
- Forty 1½" (3.8cm) nails
- Hammer

- Saw
- Drill
- ¹⁄₃₂" (0.8mm) drill bit
- ¼" (6.4mm) drill bit
- ⅜" (9.5mm) drill bit
- Small T-square or straight edge
- Ruler or tape measure
- Pencil or black marker

Step 1. Measure and cut four pieces of 12" (30.5cm) long pine boards. These four pieces will make your hotel frame.

Step 2. Use your pencil to mark three small dots on the right side of all four frame pieces, placing dots ½" (1.2cm) from each side, and placing one in the middle.

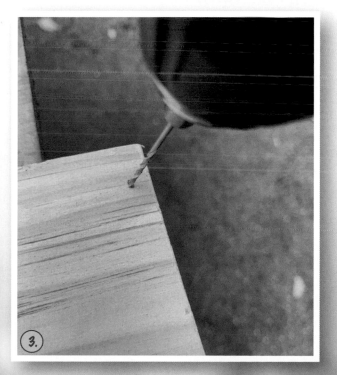

Step 3. Drill small holes where you marked the wood.

Step 4. Place a nail into each hole.

5.

Step 5. Using your hammer, pound the nails into the left side end edge of each board. Repeat until all four pieces are connected. Do not use glues or adhesives, as these can be toxic to insects and bees.

6.

Step 6. Cut a piece of pine wood to fit across the inside of the frame. This will be for your center dividers. To ensure the perfect fit, simply place the board down and draw a small mark on the inside edge. Using your straight edge, draw a line straight across, then cut along it.

7.

Step 7. On the same board, draw two lines across, spaced 3¾" (9.5cm) from each side. Mark three evenly spaced spots across each line, then drill.

Step 8. Fit the long divider piece into the frame. Do not nail it into place. Once placed in, measure the distance between it and the inside of the frame. Measure both sides.

Step 9. Next, cut two shorter dividers and nail them to your long middle divider, which will be placed horizontally. With the fully assembled middle dividers nailed together, slide them into the frame.

Step 10. Draw straight lines on the outside of the frame where the edges of the dividers meet the frame. Then, drill three holes through the frame board only, and nail it into place.

Step 11. With the remaining white pine, measure and cut two pieces to cover the back of the frame from side to side. Drill holes, then nail into place.

Step 12. Measure the inside depth of your bug house and cut bamboo and log pieces to length, making sure no pieces stick out of the frame. Then, with a drill, drill different-sized holes using your ⅜" and ¼" (9.5 and 6.4mm) drill bits in the log pieces. Drill about 5" (12.7cm) into the log pieces. Do not drill the entire way through the log.

Filling Your Bug Hotel

When filling your bug hotel, the goal is to provide as many open cavities as possible for bees and bugs to lay eggs and protect themselves from the weather. For this project, we used a collection of small pinecones, tree bark we found on fallen trees in the woods, small branches found on the ground, a piece of an old, dried-out log, and several feet of bamboo. It's important not to cut down live trees or break branches off living plants.

Step 13. When you're ready to fill your bug hotel, place the log pieces first. Surround each piece with bamboo tubes cut to the same length. Fill each compartment until all pieces are tightly against each other. Fill the small compartments with a combination of pinecones, tree bark, and twigs.

All About
Butterflies and Moths

There are about 100,000 different types of butterflies and moths around the world. They can be found on every continent except Antarctica. Butterflies and moths have many features in common. Like all insects, they have six legs. Most adults have two pairs of wings.

The great owl butterfly (above) lives in Central and South America. It has a wingspan reaching 8" (20.3cm) and can be easily identified by its huge eye spots, which resemble the eyes of an owl.

Attacus atlas (left) is the largest moth in the world. It lives in Central and South America and has a wingspan that can reach 10" (25.4cm) wide.

How is a butterfly different than a moth?

Butterfly antennae, or feelers, are slender and end in little knobs. Moth antennae lack these knobs. They often look like tiny feathers or threads. Butterfly wings are usually brightly colored or boldly patterned. Most moths have a duller color and a thicker body than butterflies. Another key difference is that butterflies are active during the daytime, while moths generally are active only at night. They're even different in how they sit still! Butterflies tend to rest with their wings in a closed, upright position, while moths rest with their wings flattened, or horizontal, to their bodies.

Did YOU KNOW ?

Unlike bees, butterflies and moths are considered accidental pollinators. They don't visit flowers for its pollen, but only for its nectar. They pick up pollen accidently when it sticks to their legs. They then carry the pollen to nearby flowers where it falls off and completes the pollination process for flowers that require cross-pollination.

The Many Stages of a Butterfly or Moth

Butterflies and moths have one very important thing in common: they both start life from an egg and hatch as a larva or caterpillar. After a period of time, the caterpillar changes into a form called a pupa. After a few weeks or months, the pupa transforms into a fully winged adult butterfly or moth. When you see a caterpillar crawling on a tree or bush, know that one day soon he or she will turn into a beautiful butterfly or moth.

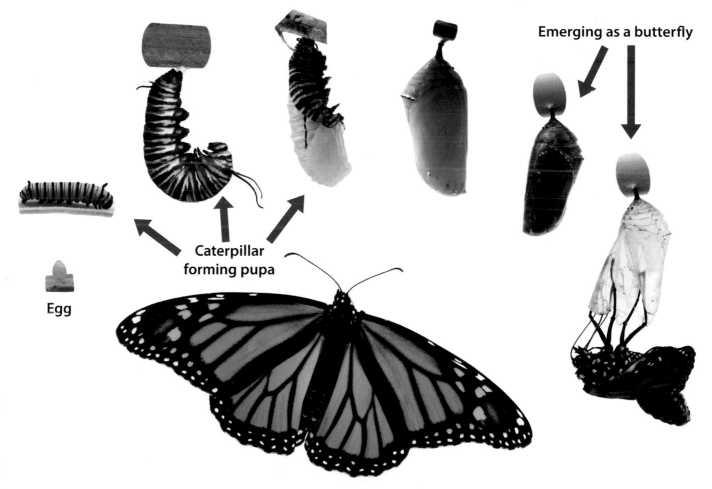

Emerging as a butterfly

Caterpillar forming pupa

Egg

The entire transformation from caterpillar to adult monarch butterfly will take 10–14 days.

Popular
Butterflies

Black swallowtail. The black swallowtail is the designated state butterfly of both New Jersey and Oklahoma. This species also has the common name of "parsnip swallowtail," named after their favorite food: the foliage and flowers of parsnips! They also feed on parsley, dill, fennel, carrot, and other similar plants.

Cabbage white. The cabbage white is one of the most widespread types of butterflies in the world. These butterflies can be found on most continents, including Asia, Europe, North America, North Africa, and Australia. It goes by multiple names. In Europe, its usual common name is the "small white." In New Zealand, it's simply called the "white butterfly." In North America and other parts of the world, the most common names include "cabbage white" and "cabbage butterfly."

Eastern tiger swallowtail. This species is native to the eastern territories of North America. It covers a geographical area spanning from parts of Canada all the way down to Florida. This butterfly is one of the most well-known species in the US. It's so admired that it's been designated the state butterfly of Alabama, North and South Carolina, Delaware, Georgia, and Virginia. They are big butterflies with a wingspan that can reach nearly 6" (15.2cm) across. They feed on multiple species of flowers but are especially attracted to red or pink ones.

Monarch. The monarch butterfly is perhaps the most well-known butterfly species in North America. Its bright wing coloring and patterns are hard to miss. It's also a very important pollinator species. While it's most common in the US, it can also be seen in southern Canada and northern South America. It's also been sighted in Papua New Guinea, Australia, New Zealand, the Philippines, Morocco, and continental Portugal.

Mourning cloak. Mourning cloak butterflies can be found throughout North America and Eurasia. It's such a popular butterfly that it's been adopted as the state insect of Montana. They prefer colder, mountainous climates and hardwood forests, but can occasionally be spotted in other geographical areas and habitats. Although rare, they can even travel down to northern South America, and further down south in more temperate regions of Eurasia. The most impressive thing about the mourning cloak is how long it lives compared to other butterflies. The mourning cloak has a lifespan of 12 months, which is longer than most other butterfly species in the world!

Orange sulfur. The orange sulfur is found throughout North America and also goes by the name "alfalfa butterfly." These butterflies are unique because their wings can reflect light in the ultraviolet range! They glow in the dark, kind of like a sulfur lamp. They're very vibrant, even compared to other butterflies.

Painted lady. The painted lady is the most widespread butterfly in the world. It can be found in any temperate zone and on every continent, except for Antarctica and South America. This butterfly prefers a warm climate, and like the monarch, partakes in a multi-generational migration between spring and autumn. Because of this, it can be sighted across the world, but during different months of the year.

Regal fritillary. The regal fritillary is a beautiful butterfly, but also a species of special concern. Due to ongoing natural habitat destruction, the regal butterfly is now confined to just a small area of the east-central US. It lives in tallgrass prairies. However, over 99% of their natural habitat has been lost. Adult butterflies feed on milkweed and thistle nectar. But these native flowers are seen as weeds and often killed with herbicides.

Viceroy. The viceroy butterfly is another very common North American species. It covers a geographic range from southern Canada, throughout the US, and down to Mexico. This species is most well-known for its remarkable similarity to the monarch butterfly. Both the monarch and the viceroy butterflies are unpalatable to predators, meaning they taste really bad to birds, who learn to avoid them. Viceroy butterflies are smaller, with a maximum wingspan of about 3" (7.6cm) and also have a black line that runs vertically across the underside of their back wings.

Long-tailed blue. The long-tailed blue lives in flowery meadows and prefers warmer temperatures. It can be found throughout Central and Southern Europe, South and Southeast Asia, Africa, and Australia. This species can also be found in Hawaii. It's a small butterfly with a wingspan just over 1" (2.5cm). Male butterflies have deep violet-blue-colored wings with soft, hairlike scales giving the wing a fuzzy appearance.

The Monarch Butterfly

Most people would agree that the Monarch butterfly is the most popular butterfly in North America, although there are a few places like Australia and New Zealand where monarchs can also be found. Monarchs are not only beautiful butterflies but are also very important pollinators who can travel amazing distances across the United States and Mexico.

Monarchs Love Milkweed Plants

If your goal is to attract and help monarchs in your area, planting milkweed is a must. Monarchs only lay their tiny eggs on the underside of milkweed leaves. The eggs are very small and poisonous to other insects or birds who might think these tiny eggs would make a great snack. Once the monarch eggs hatch, a tiny caterpillar emerges who will feed off the milkweed leaves for food. So, if you have a milkweed plant in your yard and notice leaves with pieces missing, you just might have baby monarch caterpillars somewhere on the plant. The best time to plant milkweed is in the fall. The cold temperatures and moisture from the winter months will help the plants grow in early spring. Milkweed plants, and monarchs, also like a lot of sun.

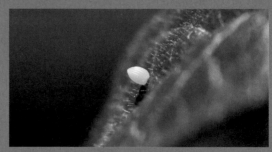

Did You KNOW ?

Monarchs taste bad to most animals and birds who might think they're a tasty treat. Their bright orange color is a warning that they not only taste bad but are also poisonous when eaten. The toxic chemical in their body comes from feeding on milkweed.

What's the difference between male and female monarchs?

All males have two small black spots on the hindwings; females do not.

Monarch's Favorite
Flowers

Goldenrod

Milkweed

Salvia

Cosmos

Lantana

Lilac

Marigold

Zinnia

A monarch butterfly searching for nectar.

How do monarchs get nectar?

Monarchs smell with their antennae. They taste water and nectar from the tiny hairs on their legs and feet. Monarchs drink through a very long tongue called a proboscis that works like an eyedropper, drawing up nectar one sip at a time. When not in use, the monarch will coil up its tongue under its lower lip.

Monarch Numbers Are in Decline

Although monarchs are very popular and admired by people of all ages, their numbers are in decline due to habitat loss, as well as extreme weather conditions and the use of pesticides over the years by people. As with all pollinators, we can also do our part to keep the monarch population strong by planting wildflowers and milkweed plants wherever and whenever we can.

The Great Monarch Migration

During cold months, most butterflies will find safe places to rest or hibernate, like cracks in rocks, tree bark, hollow trees, or anywhere that gets them out of the weather. During this time, butterflies will also slow down their internal body systems and remerge in the spring when temperatures start to rise.

Monarch Butterrfly
Fall Migration Patterns

Unlike most butterflies and insects, monarch butterflies are the only butterfly that will migrate to warmer weather in the fall months and return in the spring. This annual migration is one of nature's most mysterious and amazing events. Scientists continue to study the habits of

the monarch to better understand how this tiny, fragile insect has developed such an amazing sense of direction and ability to fly great distances.

Migration takes several generations!

Monarchs travel great distances to warmer climates in Mexico and the west coast of the United States. During the trip south, a monarch can travel up to 100 miles (160.9km) a day—or even further if the weather and wind conditions are good! Once a monarch arrives in warmer climates, the females will lay eggs to begin the next generation of monarchs. These will be the first generation to make the first part of the long trip back north. These are called Generation One and live about 2–5 weeks, traveling as far north as they can before they die. Toward the end of their lives, they will lay eggs and start a new generation who will continue the journey north. These monarchs (Generation Two) will continue to move north once they've changed from a caterpillar to butterfly. Again, they will only live about 2–5 weeks, but will lay eggs before they die, starting the third generation who will continue the same cycle, slowly moving north with each generation. Scientists believe it takes between 4–5 generations of monarchs to complete the trip north for the summer months.

The last generation, or migratory generation, of monarchs has the task of flying south for the winter and can live up to 8 months, much longer than the prior generations that made the move north. Some monarchs will fly as far as 3,000 miles (4,828km) to reach their winter home.

Monarchs will only travel during the day and will find a resting spot for the night. They gather in trees and bushes to help keep warm. These sites are called roost sites. In the mornings, monarchs will bask in the sunlight for several minutes to warm up before they start the many miles they must cover by sunset. Along the way, monarchs are always looking to refuel, stopping to fill up with nectar wherever they can find wildflowers.

Marvelous
Moths

Moths are known as great mimics in the insect world. Over thousands of years, moths have developed abilities to impersonate other animals to avoid being eaten. Some moths have evolved to look like bad-tasting insects such as wasps and praying mantises. Some moths have developed wing patterns that allow them to easily blend into their surroundings like tree bark or leaves.

Abbott's sphinx moth. Sphinx moths are among the fastest insects on Earth and have been clocked at over 30 mph (48.1kph). Because of their speed and size, they are often mistaken for hummingbirds. In fact, the most well-known sphinx moth is the hummingbird moth!

Argent and sable. The argent and sable moth has very distinctive black-and-white wings and it's found near bogs and open woodlands. This moth is found primarily in the UK region.

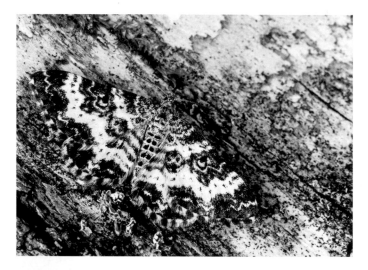

Cecropia moth. With a wingspan of 7" (17.8cm), the cecropia moth is the largest found in North America. As with most moths, they come out at night. They are found in the forests east of the Rocky Mountains in the United States and Canada.

Dagger moth. Dagger moths are named for the dagger-like mark near their upper wings. An American dagger moth can be found east of the Rocky Mountains in forests, near houses, and even in more populated places, and can live up to three years. Do not try to pick up a dagger moth! They have specialized poisonous hairs that can break off in your skin and cause a rash that will be very painful for several days.

Did You Know ?

A moth will form a cocoon around itself as a caterpillar, much like a butterfly. It will emerge later as a fully formed moth. The larval, or caterpillar, stage typically lasts about 7 weeks. The larvae are most active during the months of May and June. The individual larvae become pupae in late June on into July and remain in this stage for 1 to 2 weeks. Adults emerge in late June through the middle part of July and can persist into August.

Madagascan sunset moth. As the name suggests, this moth is native to Madagascar. The wings reflect light at different angles to add more brilliance to its many bright colors. It is also very poisonous to predators.

Luna moth. The luna moth gets its name from the word "luna," which means "moon." Luna moths born close to autumn will overwinter in their cocoons and emerge the following spring. Luna moths are not rare but are rarely seen by humans. This is due to their very brief (7–10 day) adult lives and nocturnal flying time. They are also found in forested areas throughout eastern North America, as far west as Texas, and parts of southeastern Canada.

Milionia moths. The milionia moth is found primarily in Japan and parts of the Himalayas.

Life cycle of the silk moth: egg, caterpillar, cocoon, pupae. The entire transformation will take between 65 and 90 days.

An adult silk moth.

Spanish moon moth. The Spanish moon moth is native to parts of France and Spain and is one of the most unique moths on the planet. They like dry and mountainous pine forests. They have a very short life span as adults—about a week.

White witch. The white witch is often referred to as the world's largest moth with a wingspan that can reach up to 1' (30.5cm) across. The white witch lives in the rainforests of South and Central America.

The Hummingird Moth

The hummingbird moth is not a bird, but it can easily be mistaken for a hummingbird at first glance as it hovers around flowers while searching for nectar. As with most moths, the hummingbird moth is more active in late evening and night, helping to pollinate any nearby flowers while the daytime pollinators like bees and butterflies are resting. Although not easy to see, hummingbird moths can be found throughout North America, Europe, Africa, and Asia.

Why do hummingbird moths get mistaken for hummingbirds?

Part of the reason many people can easily confuse a hummingbird moth with a hummingbird is its amazing ability to hover over flowers while searching for nectar. Hummingbird moths have a tail that can open like a fan, and the ability to beat their wings very fast, which helps them to hover in place.

Did **YOU KNOW** ?

There are four different types of hummingbird moths in North America: hummingbird clearwing moths, white-lined sphinx moths, snowberry clearwing moths, and slender clearwing moths. All share a lot of common characteristics. In addition to their ability to hover, they all have very fuzzy, thick antennae, plump bodies like bumblebees, and clear patches on their wings.

What kinds of flowers do hummingbird moths like?

Hummingbird moths like a lot of different flowers, especially phlox and bee balm. Unlike hummingbirds, hummingbird moths don't prefer red over other colors. They also like pale colors and white.

How to Tell a Hummingbird Moth from a Hummingbird

Hummingbird moths are smaller, only reaching a maximum size of about 2" (5.1cm) while hummingbirds can reach up to 4" (10.2cm) in length.

Did **YOU KNOW** ?

Hummingbird moths have an extra-long tongue, sometimes twice the length of their body. After sipping nectar from flowers, they roll their tongue up under their chin. Because of their long tongue, they can easily suck nectar from very long, tube-shaped flowers.

Bird Pollinators

A perched Cape May Warbler gets ready to eat some nectar from a cherry tree flower. Cape May Warblers are found in Canada and northern parts of the US. There are over 50 different types of warblers found throughout north and south America.

An Australian Myna bird gets nectar.

There are more than 11,000 different types of birds on the planet, but not all are considered pollinators. Within the bird world, there are six main categories of birds: perching birds, which are mostly small birds like sparrows and finches; flightless birds, such as ostriches and emus; raptors, such as eagles and hawks; seabirds, such as seagulls and terns; waterfowl, which includes ducks and swans; and what are considered specialist birds, which include penguins, woodpeckers, owls, and flamingos. Birds that are also good pollinators come from the perching group. About 2,000 different types of birds are considered pollinators. These are birds that are nectar eaters.

Compared to bees and other insects, the number of bird pollinators is very low, but they all play an important role in helping to pollinate plants. Birds help spread pollen in the same way butterflies do, picking up pollen by accident when it sticks to them as they're sucking out nectar from deep inside the flower. As they go from flower to flower, they drop pollen accidently, which helps pollinate plants that need cross-pollination.

Some of the most popular birds that help with pollination are Baltimore Orioles, honeycreepers, sunbirds, black swallowtails, and even some parrots in the rainforest. The most well-known and productive bird pollinator is the hummingbird. There are an estimated 340 different types of hummingbirds that live primarily in North and South America.

A New Holland Honeyeater feeds on a red bloom.

A European Goldfinch sits among blooming cherry blossoms.

A European Greenfinch sits on a branch.

A Purple Sunbird sits on a fence and enjoys nectar from a yellow flower. There are 132 different types of sunbirds.

A Baltimore Oriole drinks nectar from a pink-colored blossom. Baltimore Orioles have unmistakable orange-and-black coloring, and when not feeding on nectar, will also eat insects and spiders. There are about 30 different types of orioles around the world.

An American Goldfinch perched on a yellow flower.

This Rainbow Lorikeet is eating pink eucalyptus nectar. These birds have tongues that look like a paintbrush, designed for feeding on nectar. They live in rainforests and heavily wooded areas.

A young Black-headed Oriole perches on an aloe flower.

There are about 177 different types of honeyeater birds found in the forests and brushlands of Australia, New Guinea, New Zealand, and the Pacific Islands.

As nectar is a primary food source for sunbirds, they are important pollinators in African ecosystems. They are found through most of Africa to the Middle East, South Asia, Southeast Asia and southern China, Indonesia, New Guinea, and northern Australia. There are 132 different types of sunbirds.

The Golden-fronted Leafbird is a species of leafbird. It is a common resident breeder in India, Bangladesh, and parts of Southeast Asia. The Golden-fronted Leafbird eats mostly insects like worms, spiders, fruits, and nectar.

All About
Hummingbirds

Hummingbirds are the most active and important pollinators in the bird world. They are only found in the western hemisphere, which consists of North and South America and the very western parts of Europe and Africa. Hummingbirds are extremely fast flyers, and they can fly backward and sideways, which allows them to move in and out of flower blossoms quickly.

How did the hummingbird get its name?

The name "hummingbird" comes from the humming noise they make as they beat their wings.

How long do hummingbirds live?

Many hummingbirds can live up to 5 or even 10 years. A hummingbird's life span is greatly determined by the ability to find flowers producing nectar.

How fast is a hummingbird?

Hummingbirds can fly up to 23 miles (37km) a day and up to 30 mph (48.3kph). They can flap their wings from 10 to 80 times per second while hovering.

How do hummingbirds find nectar?

Believe it or not, hummingbirds have no sense of smell. They find nectar by association, that is, bright colors mean sweet nectar is near!

Hummingbirds are not only great pollinators, they also help with the summertime pests like mosquitoes. A hummingbird can consume between 700 and 1,000 insects, including mosquitoes, in a single day.

A hummingbird resting on a branch in search of insects.

A hummingbird weighs about 4 grams or .14 ounces. It would take 150 Ruby-throated Hummingbirds to make a whole pound (453.6g)!

Did You KNOW?

The legs of a hummingbird are its weakest part since most of their time is spent flying. They cannot walk or hop.

The Smallest Bird in the World

The Bee Hummingbird, which is only found in Cuba, is only 2¼" (5.7cm) long when fully grown. Bee Hummingbirds are often mistaken for bees.

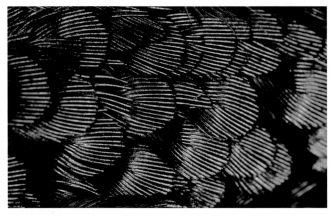

The average hummingbird has about 1,000 feathers. The colors you see depend on the angle of light when it hits the feather. Hummingbirds do not have fluffy down feathers that help keep birds warm in colder temperatures, another reason they head south for the winter.

Unlike the hummingbird, this bluebird has fluffy down feathers to keep it warm in the cold.

Hummingbirds have a very high metabolism and must eat all day long just to survive. They consume about half their body weight in bugs and nectar, feeding every 10-15 minutes and visiting 1,000–2,000 flowers throughout the day.

What do hummingbird chicks eat?

Baby hummingbirds need a high-protein diet of insects to fuel fast growth and to develop strong bones and beaks. They also need nectar to meet their high-energy needs. A mother hummingbird will leave the nest to drink nectar and eat soft-bodied bugs, including mosquitoes, gnats, spiders, caterpillars, aphids, insect eggs, fruit flies, and small bees.

Hummingbirds, and especially growing babies, need protein in their diets if they are to remain healthy. Bugs provide that protein. That they eat mosquitoes, gnats, and aphids is a great reason to try to attract hummingbirds to your backyard.

When the mother returns to the nest, the babies will feel the wind from her wings and lift their heads with open mouths to be fed. Mom inserts her beak into their mouths and regurgitates the partially digested bugs and nectar.

The mother hummingbird will return to the nest at least every 20 minutes with more food for her growing babies. The mom will fly back and forth to the nest from the nearest food source constantly for many days, almost driving herself to complete exhaustion, until her babies are ready to leave the nest and can take care of themselves.

Hummingbirds Build with Spider Webs

Hummingbird nests are very small and tucked away between branches, leaves, and even cracks in rocks. It's important to never disturb a bird's nest when you see one in nature. To help secure their nest, female hummingbirds will use pieces from nearby spider webs to help hold everything together. It takes about a week for the female hummingbird to build its nest. A hummingbird will lay two eggs, usually a day or so apart. A baby hummingbird will be ready to leave its nest about 18–24 days after hatching. So, if you want to attract hummingbirds to your garden, keep the spiders and their webs.

Did You Know?

During migration, a hummingbird's heart beats up to 1,260 times a minute, and its wings flap 15 to 80 times a second. To support this high energy level, a hummingbird will typically gain 25-40% of their body weight before they start migration in order to make the long trek over land and water.

A Hummingbird's Tongue

The tongue of the hummingbird is grooved like the shape of a *W*, which helps them pull nectar from deep inside a flower blossom. They gather nectar by moving their tongue in and out of their slender beak about 13 times per second.

A female Ruby-throated Hummingbird feeding her two chicks.

Never Disturb a Bird's Nest

A bird's nest is not only hard work for the birds to build, but also the baby birds' home and protection until they're old enough to fly on their own. Moving or disturbing a bird's nest will make it difficult for the adult birds to protect and feed their babies.

When baby hummingbirds hatch, they have no feathers and dark skin. Depending on the type or species of hummingbird, the babies will weigh approximately 0.62 grams. That's ⅓ the weight of a United States dime. They are about 1" (2.5cm) long and cannot regulate their own body heat.

Hummingbirds can fly less than a month after hatching. At around two weeks old, baby hummingbirds start exercising their wings to prepare for their initial flights. Once they are ready to fly, they leave the nest, a process called fledging.

Hummingbirds Head South for the Winter

Hummingbirds don't like the cold and will head south for the winter, with many flying to Mexico or northern Panama. Unlike many birds that fly south for the winter, hummingbirds will fly alone, so you won't see them flying in flocks. Although a hummingbird born in the spring up north has never been south, it will know instinctively that it's time to head south and know the best route to take to Mexico. Scientists who track hummingbirds have observed that a hummingbird will take the same route year after year.

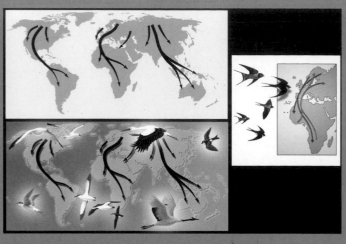

RUBY-THROATED HUMMINGBIRDS

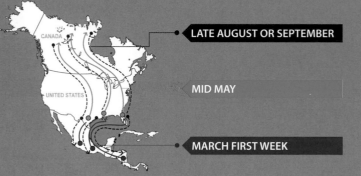

- LATE AUGUST OR SEPTEMBER
- MID MAY
- MARCH FIRST WEEK

Do hummingbirds return to the same place every year?

Hummingbirds have a fantastic memory and will return to the same feeder every year. If these feeders are not out or you've decided to not plant a flower garden again, the hummingbirds may leave to look somewhere else and never return.

Flying thousands of miles every year!

Compared to other migrating birds, hummingbirds go the farthest when you consider their tiny size. For a 2½" (6.4cm) hummingbird, the few thousand miles traveled each year is like a large bird going around the world.

The Rufous Hummingbird has the longest migration of any hummingbird species. Their annual migration path covers more than 3,000 miles from Alaska and Canada to southern Mexico. This extraordinarily long migration is 78 million times the bird's body length of 3 to 4 inches (7.6 to 10.2cm). If it were the same size as a human, the Rufous Hummingbird's migration would take it around the world three times.

What bird holds the record for longest migration recorded?

The Arctic Tern travels nearly 60,000 miles (90,000 km) every year, migrating from Greenland in the north of the Weddell Sea near Antarctica. The Artic Tern is not a pollinator but is certainly an impressive bird that continues to impress bird watchers and scientists alike.

Will you ever see a flock of hummingbirds?

Very simply, no. Unlike many birds, hummingbirds live most of their lives alone, always on the move in search of a food source. They are also very territorial and quick to scare off other hummingbirds when they find a favorite patch of flowers or a hummingbird feeder that they do not want to share.

Rufous Hummingbird. These birds are nectar feeders and prefer to stay close to flowers like lilies, mint, larkspurs, heaths, fireweed, and Indian paintbrush for the nectar and the visiting insects. They catch these insects from the air or pick them from their wings or spiderwebs. They are found in high places like mountain meadows at more than 12,000 feet (3,700m) elevation from sea level during migration. They are one of the most aggressive and angry American birds. They tirelessly chase each other, and other species of birds, off—even those that are bigger than them.

Amethyst-throated Sunangel. This hummingbird is native to South America. It is located primarily in Ecuador, Bolivia, and Peru.

Bee Hummingbird. The Bee Hummingbird is the smallest bird in the world. It's so small that it's often mistaken for an insect. It's only found in Cuba.

Anna's Hummingbird. Anna's Hummingbirds eat nectar from many flowering plants, including currant, gooseberry, and manzanita.

Cinnamon Hummingbird. This hummingbird is found in the southwestern region of Mexico and other Central American countries.

Dusky Hummingbird. These birds are native to Mexico. Both the female and males have a white stripe behind the eye.

Fork-tailed Woodnymph Hummingbird. These birds grow to about 3"–5" (7.6–12.7cm) long. They live in South American and prefer dense forests.

Giant Hummingbird. These birds can reach nearly 8" (20.3cm) in length and live in the western region of South America. They feed on nectar, insects, and the occasional spider.

Green Hermit Hummingbirds. These live primarily in the region from Panama to Costa Rica and Peru. They are easy to identify with their long, curved, reddish bill, which is perfect for sucking nectar out of tubular flowers.

Hooded Visorbearer Hummingbird. These are smaller hummingbirds only reaching 3"–4" (7.6–10.2cm) in length, with very straight, black bills. They are native to Bahia, an eastern Brazilian state.

The Long-billed Hermit. This bird has a unique long tail and very long, curved bill, which can measure over 1½" (3.8cm). The long-billed hermit lives in the eastern part of central America.

Indigo-capped Hummingbird. This bird can be found Central America and northwestern South America. It's easy to spot unless it's sitting against a bunch of green leaves. Its nearly all-green color is great camouflage when sitting in a green bush or tree.

Many-spotted Hummingbird. As the name implies, the Many-spotted Hummingbird is covered with many small, dark spots. It is found in small areas on the eastern slope of the Andes Mountains in South America.

Orange-throated Sunangel. This hummingbird has a short, straight bill. It is found in the Andes Mountains of Venezuela and eastern Columbia. They are easily identified by their bright orange throat.

Long-billed Starthroat. This is a larger hummingbird, reaching nearly 5" (12.7cm) in length. It has a very long, slightly curved bill and a small white spot behind each eye.

Purple-throated Mountaingem Hummingbird. This bird is common in the cloud forests of Nicaragua, Costa Rica, and Panama. It has a very distinctive white stripe down the side of its head.

Rufous-tailed Hummingbird. These have a distinctive rufous tail and a bright pink bill. They are very common in southern Mexico southward to northwestern South America.

Scaley-breasted Hummingbird. This bird is found in Central America, from Belize to Panama and northern Colombia. They have a black bill with a little pink toward the base.

Sapphire-bellied Hummingbird. These have a forked tail and can only be found on the Atlantic coast of Colombia. Its favorite place to live is in tropical mangrove forests.

Tawny-bellied Hermit. These hummingbirds are found in the mountains of Colombia, Ecuador, and Peru in their very humid forests. They have a very long, curved bill. As with many hummingbirds, they will revisit the same food sources on a very regular basis.

Volcano Hummingbird. This bird is very small, only about 3" (7.6cm) in length. Volcano Hummingbirds can be found in the very high mountain slopes and volcanoes of Costa Rica and Panama.

Red-billed Streamertail Hummingbird. This is one of the most unique hummingbirds on the planet. It is found throughout Jamaica and has a bright red bill and extremely long tail feathers.

White-whiskered Hermit Hummingbird. Despite its name, this bird does not have actual whiskers. Instead, they have very bold stripes above and below their eyes. They live in regions of Colombia and Ecuador.

Xantu's Hummingbirds. These are native to the southern part of Baja, California. They are very small and hard to spot in nature, as many of their colors are earth tones.

How to Build a
Hummingbird Feeder

A hummingbird feeder has three basic parts: a reservoir to hold your homemade nectar, a tube where the hummingbird can suck nectar from, and a red, flower-like object that will draw their attention in flight.

You will need:

- One clean glass bottle with plastic cap. Bottles made to hold cooking sauces like soy sauce make great containers for hummingbird feeders.
- One clean plastic water or soda bottle
- One bendy straw (red or pink color)
- Red paint (acrylic spray)
- 4' (1.2m) plastic coated wire
- Superglue
- Scissors
- Drill and drill bit the same size as straw diameter
- Black marker

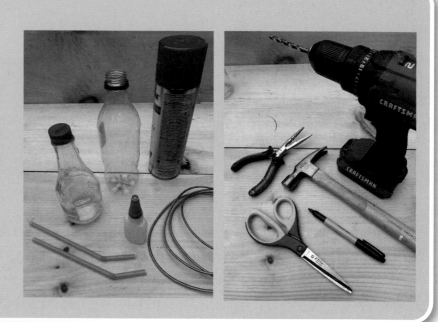

Beware Red Dye

Some birds, like the Ruby-throated Hummingbird, prefer orange or red flowers. Despite this, red dye should not be used in nectar, as it could harm the birds. Instead, plant naturally red or orange flowers or use feeders that have red coloring in their structure.

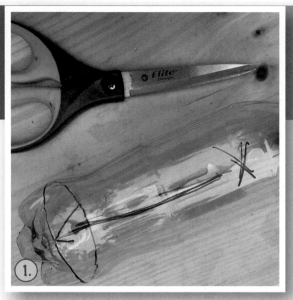

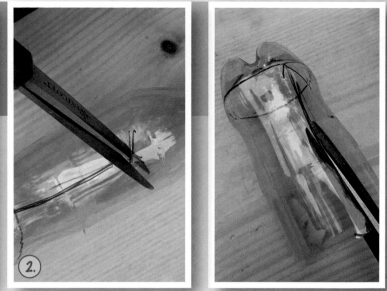

Step 1. Using your black marker, draw a line about 1" (2.5cm) from the bottom of the plastic bottle. Then, draw a straight line up the side, and a final line around the top of the bottle.

Step 2. Carefully push the tips of your scissors into the side of the bottle. Cut the top off, then cut down the side of the bottle.

Step 3. Make a final cut, following the line 1" (2.5cm) from the bottom of the bottle.

Step 4. Form a flower shape by cutting out five *V* shapes around the side.

Step 5. Drill a hole in the center of the plastic bottle bottom. Make sure the hole is the same size as the straw.

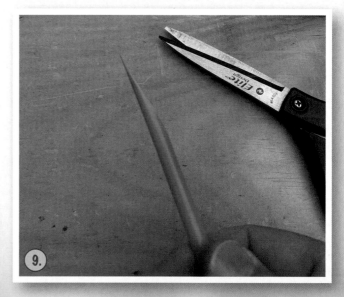

Step 6. Paint the outside with red acrylic paint. Allow to dry following the instructions on the label.

Step 7. While the paint is drying on the plastic bottom piece, remove the plastic cap from the glass bottle and drill a hole through the center. It's important the hole is the same diameter as the bendy straw. The straw used in this project has a ¼" (6.4mm) diameter.

Step 8. Cut the long side of the straw to form a point, which will make it easier to insert in the bottle cap and plastic red bottle bottom.

Step 9. Insert the pointed side of the straw through the red plastic flower, pulling the straw through until the bendy part is on the back side of the flower.

Step 10. Next, pull the straw through until the cap is ¼" (6.4mm) before the bendy part of the straw.

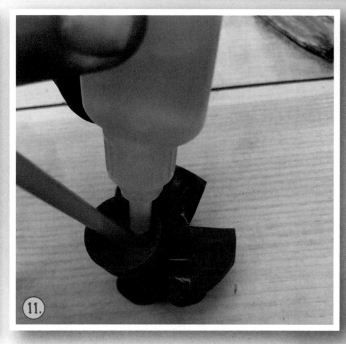

Step 11. Once the cap is in place as shown, superglue around the straw and let it dry. The glue will act as a seal and prevent the nectar from leaking.

Step 12. Take your rubber-coated wire and form a loop on one end.

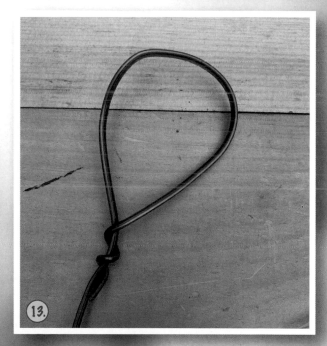

Step 13. From the loop, leave about 8"–10" (20.3–25.4cm) of straight wire leading to the center of glass bottle.

Step 14. Bend the wire across the bottle and down the side. Wrap the wire around the bottle at least twice, keeping it tight around the bottle until you reach the neck.

Step 15. Take the remaining wire and wrap it once toward the bottom of bottle, twisting around the straight piece coming down from the loop. Cut off any extra with wire-cutting pliers.

Finding the Perfect Place for Your Hummingbird Feeder

Hummingbirds are always on the lookout for sweet nectar, as well as places to rest when not hovering in front of a flower bloom or flying from plant to plant. Place your hummingbird feeder within 10'–12' (3–3.7m) of a tree, tall shrub, or a place on your front porch or deck that the bird can rest and conserve energy when not eating nectar.

Avoid full sun. Hummingbirds prefer shady areas and staying cool during the day. A hummingbird feeder placed in full sun will not see many visitors.

Hang your hummingbird feeder at least 5'–6' (152.4–182.9cm) off the ground and at least 2'–3' (61–91.4cm) from other objects. Hummingbirds are very cautious birds and like to have a quick way to fly in and out without other objects in the way.

16.

Step 16. Fill your bottle with the homemade nectar to about 2" (5.1cm) from the top. Screw the cap with straw and red flower onto the bottle and turn it over. You will see the nectar start to come down the straw and drip a little bit. If no nectar comes down, turn the bottle back over and dump out a little bit of the sugar water, about ¼" (6.4mm) at a time. Screw the straw and flower back on and try again. The amount of air in the bottle will help push the water down the straw but not completely out unless the hummingbird sucks out the nectar with its long tongue.

How to Make Nectar for Your Hummingbird Feeder

Mix one part sugar with four parts water (for example, one cup of sugar with four cups of water) until the sugar is dissolved. Do not add red dye. Extra sugar water can be stored in a refrigerator. Empty out your feeder every other day and replace with fresh sugar water.

Beetles

Ladybird Beetle

Even with all the good work done by bees and butterflies, beetles actually make up the largest group of pollinating insects. Scientists have discovered over 350,000 different types of beetles and there are more waiting to be discovered. Some bug experts believe there could be as many as 3 million different types of beetles living on the planet. They are responsible for pollinating 88% of the 240,000 flowering plants around the world! Their numbers are so big that one out of every four animals on Earth is a beetle.

Beetles Live Everywhere

You can find beetles almost anywhere on the planet, on every continent (except Antarctica), and living in every type of climate and terrain, from hot deserts to cold and windy mountains. Archaeologists have found beetles in fossils dating back 270 million years. Beetles are tough and have adapted to live in the harshest conditions and environments on the planet.

Longhorn Beetle

Soldier Beetle

Did YOU KNOW ?

Beetles can both hurt and help the environment. Some beetle species destroy crops or property, while some species help get rid of garbage, eat dead trees, or help pollinate flowers.

Ladybird Beetle

Some beetles are not considered pests. Ladybugs are beetles and are considered to be good luck in many cultures. Fireflies and lightning bugs are also beetles. They glow in the dark to communicate.

What flowers do beetles like?

Beetles are not overly picky and can be found on a wide range of flowers gathering pollen or nectar. Among their many favorites are golden rod, spirea, spicebush, yarrow, and sunflowers.

Quick Beetle Facts

Adult beetles have two sets of wings.

Most beetles only live for a year.

Beetles are found on land and in fresh water and can adapt to almost any environment.

Beetles usually just live where they eat.

Beetles cannot see very well, so they communicate using smell, sounds, or vibrations.

Longhorn Beetle

Ladybugs

If there was a popularity contest among beetles, the ladybug would win. They are one of the most loved insects around the world and are found on every continent except Antarctica. There are over 5,000 different types of ladybugs, with 450 being native to the United States.

Where do ladybugs live?

Their favorite flowers include geraniums, cosmos, fennel, and tansy.

That's Fast

Ladybugs can fly and reach speeds up to 37 mph (59.5 kph) and go over 3,000 feet (914 meters) in the sky. Just before takeoff, a ladybug will lift its shell and unfold its two pair of wings, which they can flap up to 85 times per second. Although they are fast, they make short trips when flying, often only a few minutes.

Did You KNOW ?

Not all ladybugs are red with black spots. Ladybugs can also be yellow, orange, brown, pink, and even all black. Some ladybugs don't have spots, but instead have markings more like stripes, or no markings at all.

Pest Control

Ladybugs are not only great little pollinators, but they are a gardener's best friend. Along with eating pollen as a favorite food, they also eat aphids, which are tiny organisms that can damage plants. Rose bushes are a common plant that attracts aphids. If you see ladybugs on your rose bushes, know they are hard at work eating the aphids—and, of course, visiting the bloom for pollen. An adult ladybug can eat as many as 5,000 aphids in its lifetime.

Types of Ladybugs

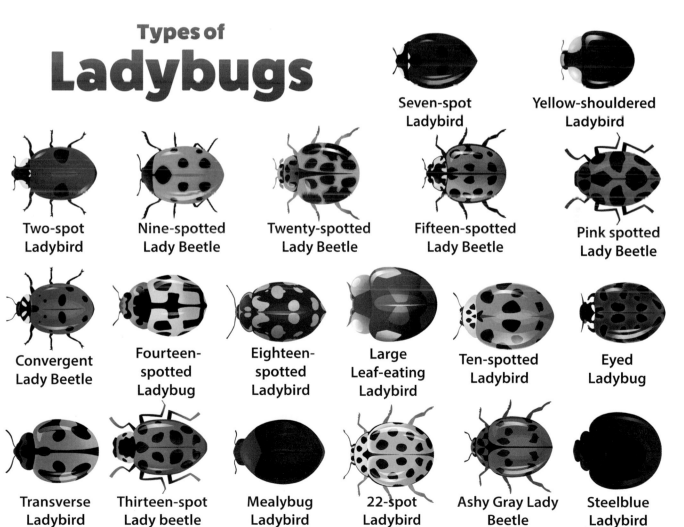

Seven-spot Ladybird

Yellow-shouldered Ladybird

Two-spot Ladybird

Nine-spotted Lady Beetle

Twenty-spotted Lady Beetle

Fifteen-spotted Lady Beetle

Pink spotted Lady Beetle

Convergent Lady Beetle

Fourteen-spotted Ladybug

Eighteen-spotted Ladybird

Large Leaf-eating Ladybird

Ten-spotted Ladybird

Eyed Ladybug

Transverse Ladybird

Thirteen-spot Lady beetle

Mealybug Ladybird

22-spot Ladybird

Ashy Gray Lady Beetle

Steelblue Ladybird

Hoverflies

Hoverflies, sometimes called flower flies, are great pollinators. They get their name from their ability to hover over flowers when searching and feeding on nectar. There are over 6,000 different types of hoverflies around the world.

How to Spot a Hoverfly

Hoverflies are often mistaken for bees or wasps. The quickest way to know the difference is watching how they fly. Bees and wasps have very little ability to hover in place for very long. Also, the hoverflies have very short antennae compared to wasps.

What do hoverflies eat?

Adult hoverflies feed a lot on nectar and pollen from flowers. The also eat aphids.

How long do hoverflies live?

An adult hoverfly with fully formed wings will live for 3–4 weeks.

Did YOU KNOW?

Hoverflies can keep up with the hummingbird when maneuvering around flowers. They have the ability to fly backwards, which allows them easily fly around and in flower blossoms.

Are hoverflies dangerous?

Despite their sometimes-aggressive looks, they do not sting or bite. They are harmless to people and play an important role moving pollen from one plant to another during the spring and summer seasons.

What plants do hoverflies like?

They can be found visiting a large range of flowers but especially like carrot blossoms and plants from the mint family.

135

Longhorn Beetles

Longhorn beetles, also known as longicorns, make up one of the largest groups of beetles. There are over 36,000 different types that can be found around the world. They are easy to identify, as most have extremely long antennae, often as long as or longer than the beetle's own body. Like most bees, many types of longhorn beetles love to feed on the pollen found in different types of flowers, such as sunflowers, daises, and black-eyed Susans.

Longhorn Beetle

Flower Longhorn Beetle

Did You KNOW?

There are some longhorn beetles that are very destructive, including the Asian longhorn beetle, which threatens hardwoods found in North America. The beetle is native to China and the Korean Peninsula.

Alpine Longhorn Beetle

Flower Longhorn Beetle

Longhorn Beetle

How long do longhorn beetles live?

Most longhorn beetles can live up to 60 days and like to live in dense woodlands and forests.

Longhorn Beetle

Bats and Four-Legged Pollinators

Most people don't think of bats when they think of pollinators, but they are also vital. There are over 1,400 different types of bats worldwide. Bats can be found on nearly every part of the planet except for extreme deserts and polar regions.

Did YOU KNOW ?

The large flying fox bats are also important pollinators of the eucalyptus plant found in dry Australian forests.

Quite an Appetite!

Scientists have discovered that some small bats can catch up to 1,000 or more small insects in a single hour, including pesky mosquitoes.

How big are bats?

Bats range greatly in size. The Kitti's Hog-nosed Bat (also called the bumble bat) weighs less than a penny and is the world's smallest mammal. The largest bats in the world are called flying foxes. They have wingspans up to 6' (1.8m) across.

Kitti's Hog-nosed Bat

Flying Fox

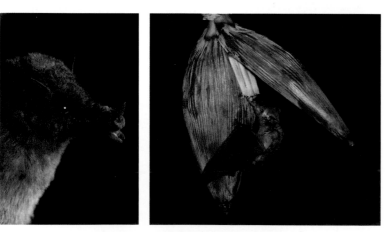
Mexican Long-tongued Bat

How to Spot Nectar-Feeding Bats

Nectar-feeding bats have some distinct features from other types of bats including a longer snout, long, brush tipped tongue, and smaller teeth. All nectar bats have a great sense of smell, which helps lead them to flowers in the dark night.

A Lesser Long-nosed Bat feeding on an agave blossom at night.

Did YOU KNOW ?

Just like the hummingbird, the Lesser Long-nosed Bat can hover over flowers and then use its 3-inch-long (7.6cm) tongue to feed on the flower's nectar. There are at least 500 different types of plants that rely on bats to help with pollination.

Fruit Bats

Without bats, bananas, avocados, and mangoes would not exists. There are over 300 types of fruit that would struggle to exist without bats to help with pollinatlon.

Did YOU KNOW ?

Baby bats are called pups, and a group of bats is a colony.

Some Bats Like Nectar

The most popular bats who feed on nectar are the Lesser Long-nosed Bat and the Mexican Long-tongued Bat. Both migrate north every spring from Mexico to the Southwest region of the United States. Both types of bats not only search for sweet nectar in flowers but are also known to feed on hummingbird feeders along the way.

A mother Short-nosed Fruit Bat rests while holding her baby on a banana flower.

A family of short-nosed or common fruit bats hides under a green, leafy palm tree during the daytime.

Creatures of the Night

Bats, like moths, are pollinators that work at night and are generally attracted to white petals, flowers with a strong smell, and flowers that open at night.

139

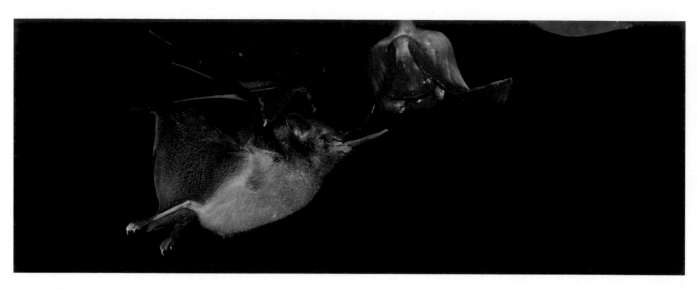

The Pallas Long-tongued Bat lives in South and Central America. It uses its very long tongue to gather nectar from blossoms at night.

Did You KNOW?

The flowers of certain types of plants, like sugarbushes, are uniquely adapted to pollination by small rodents like spiny mice.

Birds and many insects don't like sugarbush nectar because it's too sweet, but it turns out small rodents love the sweet stuff.

The Largest Pollinator in the World

No, it's not a giant bee or huge bird, it's the lemur! The black-and-white ruffed lemurs are the largest pollinators on Earth. Other lemur pollinators include dwarf lemurs, mongoose lemurs, and red-ruffed lemurs. Red-ruffed lemurs eat a diet of fruit and pollen. When they stick their noses into flowers for nectar, pollen collects on their snouts, and they transfer it from flower to flower.

On the island of Madagascar, black-and-white-ruffed lemurs are also the main pollinators of traveler's trees or traveler's palm. These trees are typically 40' (12.2m) high. The lemurs use their nimble hands to pull open the tough flowers. They stick their long snouts and tongues deep inside a tree's flower.

There are over 100 different types of lemurs, only found on the African island of Madagascar and some tiny surrounding islands.

Besides humans, lemurs are one of the only primates to have blue eyes.

Lemurs are not good swimmers and avoid water. But they can jump as far as 25' (7.6m) in one leap.

A lemur hangs from a branch.

A green gecko climbs around a torch ginger flower.

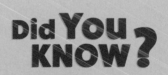

Did You KNOW?

Scientists believe that around 40 reptile species—such as lizards, geckos, and skinks—can help pollinate flowers, as well. For many small lizards, nectar is important during the dry season. While drinking the nectar, pollen may get stuck to their scales and get brushed off when they visit the next flower.

Index

Shutterstock.com Photo Credits

Front cover: *top* Daniel Prudek *middle* Rabbitti *bottom left* yuqun *bottom right* AlexandrMusuc **page 2:** phichak **page 3:** *middle right* Tanika_Pict *bottom left* Five-Birds Photography *bottom middle* xradiophotog *top* Daniel Prudek **page 6:** *background* FrentaN *top right* nobeastsofierce *top middle* los_jan *bottom right* kavcicm *middle right* baismartin **page 7:** *background* FrentaN *top left* cpaulfell *bottom left* Kevin Collison *top right* Larry Barrett **page 8:** *background* FrentaN *top right* Anton Kozyrev *bottom right* Kevin Collison **page 9:** *bottom right* David Havel *top right* Paul Sparks *top left* Diyana Dimitrova *bottom left* Keneva Photography *bottom right, top* Hatri Bidik *middle right* Dario Hipo Wild Photo **page 10:** background Marie C. Fields **page 11:** *bottom left* Juan Gaertber *top right* nobeastsofierce **page 12:** *top right* J J Osuna Caballero *bottom, background* Khorzhevska *top, background* StockImageFactory.com *bottom right* Lightspring *middle right* Elizaveta Galitckaia **page 13:** *bottom* Ondrej Prosicky *top left* Krill Demchenko **page 14:** *background* carlosramos1946 **page 15:** AllFlower Studio **page 16:** *top right* Petr Ganaj *middle right* cherryyblossom *bottom right* Eve Tran *middle left* Wirestock Creators *bottom left* Kuttelvaserova Stuchelova **page 17:** *middle right* CAGPhotography *top left* Pamela Weston **page 18:** *background* Sri J *bottom left* White Space Illustrations **page 19:** *top right* Gert-Jan van Vliet **page 20:** *bottom, background* Bits and Splits *top, background* Khorzhevska *bottom left* OtZatO **page 21:** *top left* nobeastsofierce *middle left* Olena Ukhova **page 22:** *middle left* Elena Masiutkina *top right* Pressmaster *bottom left* masterpiece creator **page 23:** *bottom* Pressmaster *top right* Pressmaster **page 24:** *bottom right, top* Matt Jeppson *top right, bottom* VMPhotoshoots *top right* mehmetkrc *bottom right* Birdiegal **page 25:** *bottom right* Minko Peev *bottom left* ThomasLENNE *top warmer* **page 26:** *middle right* aga7ta *bottom right* Kazakova Maryia *background* zlikovec **page 27:** *middle right* Lucky-photographer *middle left* jurgal *bottom right* Avalepsap *top right* KPG-Payless **page 28:** *bottom left* Lapa Smile *bottom right* Travelly Minimalist *top, background* ventdusud **page 29:** *bottom left* Happy Dragon *top left* pisaphotography *top right* Andrew Zarivny *bottom right* Frans Block **page 30:** *middle left* JayPierstorff *top, background* LHBLLC *bottom left* George Burba *top left* A. La Canfora *bottom right* Lori Bonati **page 31:** *middle left* MelaniWright *bottom right* Larry Barrett *middle right* Pi-Lens **page 32:** *bottom right* Kokhanchikov *bottom, background* Sara Winter *top left* Bob Pool **page 33:** *top* middleitsajoop *top left, bottom* Georgina198 *top right* kris *top* Kristopher ulley *top left, top* branislavpudar **page 34:** *bottom right* Wirestock Creators *bottom left* AlexanderZam: *middle right* Yarygin *top left* PhotoTrippingAmerica **page 35:** *bottom* Laura Simons *top left* Cora Mueller *top right, top* vallefrias *top right, bottom* Ton Photographer 4289 **page 36:** *middle right, bottom* Smileus *bottom, background* agrofruti *top right* varuna *top right, bottom* Iryna Nazarova **page 37:** *middle left* I Wayan Sumatika *top left, right* MakroBetz *middle right* Slatan *top left, left* Vitaliy Kyrychuk **page 38:** *middle right, top* Bukhta Yurii *bottom middle* KatMoy *top right* Brent Hofacker *middle middle* kobeza *bottom left, top* Tim UR *bottom right, bottom* Tim UR *bottom right, top* Africa Studio *bottom left* Tim UR **page 39:** *middle left* BirdShutterB *bottom middle* Sergiy Kuzmin *bottom right* nblx *bottom right, top* Kotcha K *bottom left, bottom* Anna Hoychuk *bottom middle, top* grey_and *middle middle* Yeti studio *middle right* Iaroshenko Maryna *top right*

Tatjana Baibakova *top middle* Nattiko *top left* Luiza Kamalova **page 40:** *bottom* Kq333 **page 40:** *top left* Kateryna Pavliuk **page 41:** *bottom* Pav-Pro Photography Ltd *top left* fernandoalonsostockfilms **page 42:** *bottom right* Izzie Bella *top, background* rustamank *middle left* MJANaturePics **page 43:** *top right* Steven Ellingson *bottom* RukiMedia *top left* Gerald A. DeBoer **page 44:** *top right* tomfotorama *bottom* Ant Clausen *background* kzww Leftlan 2010 *bottom middle* Min C. Chiu **page 45:** *bottom right* Pike-28 *bottom right, in circle* seecreateimages *top right* baismartin *left* jane balak **page 46:** *middle right* JuliaHermann *bottom* Freesia21 *top left* Nicola Simoncini **page 47:** *bottom right* ArtEvent ET *top right* Petr Ganaj *top left* karen crewe *bottom left* Pablo Joanidopoulos **page 48:** *bottom right* Kim McGrew *top* Printemps PhotoArt *bottom left* Supachai Rattanarueangdech **page 49:** *top* knelson20 *bottom left* Mr. Witoon Boonchoo *bottom right* Bubushonok **page 50:** *top right* Nancy Bauer *bottom left* Five-Birds Photography *bottom right* Joel Trick *top left* LR Infinity Photography **page 51:** *top left* I. Rottlaender *bottom* Kovalyk Artur *top right* Meandering Nature's Trail **page 52:** *bottom right* Tatyana Mi *bottom left* Jerry Gantar *top* nanoman **page 53:** *right* Kevin Collison *bottom left* Postshutter **page 54:** *middle left* David Byron Keener *bottom left* Jay Gao *bottom right* Christopher Unsworth *top right* KellyNelson **page 55:** *background* yanikap *top right* Sean Lema *middle left* Jon Osumi *bottom right* xradiophotog *top left* Danita Delimont **page 56:** *bottom right* Elena Zajchikova *top right* irin-k **page 57:** *top right* phichak **page 58:** *top right* Anatoly Maslennikov **page 59:** *top right* Besjunior *bottom* Shaiith *top left* Martha Marks **page 60:** *right, in box* Estragon *middle left* Mari-Leaf **page 61:** *bottom left* Todor Stoyanov *top* VectorMine: *middle left* Mircea Costina *bottom left, top* StGrafix **page 62:** *bottom right* Elliotte Rusty Harold *top right* Camyoshi *middle left* Bruce MacQueen **page 63:** *top left* kim takhyz-sviridov *bottom left* Paul Reeves Photography **page 64:** *middle left* Ralf Liebhold *bottom right* Wirestock Creators *top right* Tanika_Pict **page 65:** *top left* Paul Reeves Photography *middle right* Glenn McCrea **page 65:** *bottom left* Hwall **page 66:** *bottom* StockMediaSellee *background* tavizta **page 68:** *middle* Gayash_98 *top right, bottom* irin-k *bottom, in box* Pretty Vectors *bottom* Diyana Dimitrova *top right, top* Dani Vincek **page 69:** *top middle* DONOT6_STUDIO *top right* irin-k *top left* Charlermpon Poungpeth *bottom right* Protasov AN **page 70:** *middle three pictures* Kuttelvaserova Stuchelova *bottom, background* Igori_K *top left* Eric Isselee *top right* Chris Moody **page 71:** *top right, both* J. Marini *top* Lotus_studio **page 72:** *top, background* nnattalli *bottom left* Chris Moody *middle left* gertvansanten **page 73:** *top right* Ivaschenko Roman *bottom left* Cornel Constantin *middle* Jaroslav Moravcik **page 74:** *bottom* Yuttana Joe *top right* Ed Phillips **page 75:** *top* Jennifer Bosvert *bottom* thatmacroguy *top* Lillusion **page 80:** guentermanaus **page 81:** *bottom left* BernadetteB **page 88:** *bottom right, bottom* Kletr *bottom right, top* Jirasak Chuangsen *middle left* Cocos.Bounty *top right* Deborah Ferrin **page 89:** Kim Howell **page 90:** *middle right* Ger Bosoma Photos *bottom left* Danita Delimont *top left* Sari Oneal **page 91:** *top right* Kate Besler *bottom* Danita Delimont **page 92:** *top right* Jason Patrick Ross *middle left* Mircea Costina *bottom right* Nancy Bauer **page 93:** *bottom right* Stephan Morris *top* Paul Reeves Photography **page 94:** *top left* nanoman *bottom right, top* Maria T. Hoffman *middle right* Mariola Anna S. *bottom right, bottom* HHelene **page 95:** Media Marketing **page 96:** *top left* Nancy

Bauer *top right* Nancy Bauer *middle left* Leema Robinson *middle right* Ratda *bottom left* LedyX *bottom right* KRIACHKO OLEKSII *background* kzww

page 97: *top* Dominique Bradette *bottom left* xradiophotog *middle right* Paul Sparks **page 98:** *top* Bob Hilscher *bottom right* Map Resources *bottom left* Dotted Yeti **page 99:** IrinaK **page 100:** *middle right* P_vaida *bottom left* David Havel *top left* Karel Block **page 101:** *middle right* Landshark1 *bottom right* Mark Brandon *top left* Barry and Carole Bowden **page 102:** *bottom left* ChameleonsEye *bottom right* ozgur kerem bulur *top left* Kevin Collison *middle right* forest71 **page 103:** *top* Andreas Weitzmann *bottom* RealityImages *top right* Aleksandr Burukhin *bottom, background* aaltair **page 104:** *bottom left* Elliotte Rusty Harold **page 105:** *bottom* Cornel Constantin *top left* Bildagentur Zoonae GmbH *middle left* Karel Block **page 106:** *top right* Pics by Chris Richardson *top left* Pierre Williot **page 107:** *top* Leanne Irwin *bottom left* godi photo *bottom right* godi photo **page 108:** *top left* Gandiv *bottom left* BaadCho *bottom right* Alan Dunn *top right* Guoqiang Xue **page 109:** *bottom left* Jrs Jahangeer *top right* Martin Pelanek *bottom right* Jyotirmoy Golder *top left* Jurgens Potgieter **page 110:** *top left* Matt Knoth *top left* Matt Knoth *middle left* Dank Pics *bottom right* KellyNelson **page 111:** *middle right* J. Esteban Berrio *top right* Kwangmoozaa *bottom* xradiophotog *top left* Melody Mellinger **page 112:** *bottom left* TERRESTRE *bottom right* Lmortell *top* spatuletail **page 113:** *bottom* Freebilly Photography *top* Dec Hogan **page 114:** *top left* Scp Photop graphy **page 115:** *top* Agnieszka Bacal *bottom right* Om_Joshi *bottom left* Damsea **page 116:** *top* Amadeu Blasco *bottom* Tom Middleton **page 117:** *bottom* Ramona Edwards *top* Petr Simon **page 118:** *bottom left* spatuletail *top left* Menno Schaefer *bottom left* Keneva Photography *top right* Traveller MG **page 119:** *top left* Ondrej Prosicky *top right* tferka *bottom right* Peder Bjurke Ihle *bottom left* Ondrej Prosicky **page 120:** *top right* Ondrej Prosicky *bottom left* Martin Pelanek *middle right* Andrew M. Allport *middle left* Rafael Cerqueira **page 121:** *bottom right* Martin Pelanek *top right* Paul Wittet *top left* David Havel *middle left* Edgloris Marys **page 122:** *bottom* Ondrej Prosicky *middle left* Julio Salgado *top right* Agami Photo Agency *top middle* Tomas Drahos **page 123:** *middle right* Milan Zygmunt *bottom left* Agami Photo Agency *top right* Ondrej Prosicky *top left* Sujatha Vempaty **page 124:** *bottom* Birdiegal **page 130:** *top left* BUFOTO *middle right* Chloe Langton *bottom left* Peter van Dam **page 131:** *right* IJPhoto *left* Hamid Rustanto **page 132:** *left* Aleksandr Rybalko *right* Protasov AN **page 133:** *top right* IRGOOFY **page 134:** *bottom* left Dennis Jacobsen *middle left* Victor Scharnhorst *page top right* Daniel Wussow **page 135:** *bottom right* nounours *bottom left* Kristof Degreef *top right* Lee Corey Photography **page 136:** *bottom right* Stefan Rotter *top* SIMON SHIM *bottom left* Keith Hider **page 137:** *top left* Hwall *top right* OlegD *bottom* Hatri Bidik **page 138:** *bottom left* svaldvard *middle right* Erik Zandboer *middle left* Amarisa M *bottom right* Milan Zygmunt **page 139:** *top left* Danita Delimont *middle right* I Wayan Sumatika *bottom left* Linda_K **page 140:** *top* Martin Pelanek *bottom left* Hurly D'souza *middle left* Marion Smith-Byers *bottom right* Paul Tymon *top* David Havel **page 141:** *bottom left* mhgstan *top right* Zkye **pages 4, 56–58, 77–86, 124–128:** *background* DRubi **back cover:** *bottom left* irin-k *bottom right* Danita Delimont *middle right* karen crewe *background* DRubi

144